THE FINGER OF GOD IN THE MUSLIM WORLD

THE LIFE STORY OF MISSIONARY
ARLENE MILLER

ARLENE MILLER

WITH

MARCIA RUTH DAY ANDERSON

Cherohala Press
Cleveland, Tennessee

The Finger of God in the Muslim World
The Life Story of Missionary Arlene Miller

Published by Cherohala Press, an imprint of CPT Press
900 Walker ST NE
Cleveland, TN 37311
USA
email: cptpress@pentecostaltheology.org
website: www.cptpress.com

ISBN: 9781953358004

Copyright © 2021 CPT Press
All rights reserved. No part of this book may be reproduced or translated in any form, by print, photoprint, microfilm, microfiche, electronic database, internet database, or any other means without written permission from the publisher.

Scripture taken from the New King James Version. Copyright @1982 by Thomas Nelson, Inc. Used by permission. All rights reserved.

The cover photo shows the Dedo de Deus (The Finger of God), a mountain peak in the Serra do Mar near the southern coast of Brazil.

This book is dedicated to Dr Robert Douglas.[1]
'Thanks for being a professor *par excellence*, barring none, who also became a very dear friend. You helped me very much and sent me some extremely funny cards when I really needed a lift. Thank you, dear friend.'

Arlene Miller
Meadowbrook Care Center
Cincinnati, Ohio
July 3, 2019

---

[1] The reader will hear much more about Dr Douglas, Arlene's teacher and mentor, director of the Zwemer Institute for Muslim Studies (PhD, University of Southern California, 1980, in Religion and Social Ethics), who encouraged her greatly as she prepared to work in South America.

Contents

Foreword ix
Acknowledgements xii

Chapter 1
Chocolates and Mushrooms 1

Chapter 2
Meadowbrook Care Center 4

Chapter 3
Getting Started 9

Chapter 4
The West Bank Village of Aboud 23

Chapter 5
Aboud Primary School 36

Chapter 6
Aboud Church and Sunday School 48

Chapter 7
Transition 53

Chapter 8
Itinerating in Grief 60

Chapter
South America 61

Chapter 10
Final Reflections 82

In Memoriam 89

Tributes to Arlene Miller 94

Appendix A: Zwemer Institute for Muslim Studies 103

Appendix B: An Apologetic for Muslim Ministry 105

Appendix C: A Brief History of Islam 112

Appendix D: Muslim Social Institutions 114
Appendix E: Islamic Theology 116
Appendix F: Muslim/Arab Customs and Traditions 118
Appendix G: Students from the Missionary Training Center 122
Appendix H: Curricula at the Missionary Training Center 127

Foreword

I remember sitting in class at Fuller Theological Seminary, hearing women weeping, broken, as they shared their stories of how their churches did not value their ministry, sharing examples of discrimination by their leadership. I admit that I was confused and not a little bit angry, because we had found that single people serving on the mission field were a tremendous asset! I wanted to invite all those women to come to the mission field where there was plenty of room for workers in the harvest! Both married women and single women can make a great impact in missions – they always have in the past and they always will in the future!

The greatest influence on our family and ministry in Brazil was Arlene Miller. We had the privilege of working with her for 16 years (1994 until her accident in 2009). Arlene had previously been in Israel for 20 years working with the Palestinian people. She came to work with us in our cross-cultural training center. Our program trained American youth for missions, but we later transitioned to training Latin American candidates in 1999-2000. Arlene Miller first visited in 1994 and taught several classes while she observed our training program in preparation for the following year. From that time on, she became an essential element of our training process for cross-cultural ministry.

Arlene Miller was one of the few people in our fellowship who truly understood the need for cross-cultural training for Latin Americans. Missionaries from Latin America had served in other countries for years. Some were very successful, but others repeated the same cultural mistakes that American missionaries had made in the past before adequate training was available. Arlene not only made suggestions on improving our training program, but she also provided an essential focus on reaching the unreached people groups.

Arlene understood the strategic importance of training Latin American missionaries. Since they come from countries and cultures that are non-threatening, these missionaries could go to countries where American missionaries are not accepted. Furthermore, we found that many of the young people that God was calling in Latin

America felt a specific call to reach the Muslim people groups. Arlene was prepared to train them both through her theoretical knowledge of ministry to Muslims and through 20 years of personal experience.

The result of her ministry and that of the Missionary Training Center (MTC) in São Paulo, Brazil, is evidenced by many of the 116 Latin American missionaries serving around the world – sent out and supported by the churches and missions departments of Latin America (2018). Many of these Church of God missionaries were trained at MTC and influenced by Arlene Miller. Still others are serving as missionaries with other denominations and sending churches. Beyond the missionaries on the field, Arlene helped train countless missions leaders for the emerging missions departments, pastors and seminary students, seminary professors, and missions mobilizers that communicate the vision for missions all over Latin America. Beyond her work at MTC, Arlene traveled regularly to teach and preach in seminaries and Bible Schools, missions conferences, and local churches all over South America. The altars were always filled with young people who felt a call to missions. Her testimony spoke very strongly to others.

I would highlight four key things that I observed during our years with Arlene Miller: First, she was a dedicated evangelist. She had first initiated her ministry as a state evangelist, and as a missionary she was always seeking out the Muslim people groups in every city where she went. She had a love for the people and a passion for reaching the unreached. She not only visited the Arab churches in São Paulo, but she also actively sought out Muslim families in every city where she visited, building friendships with families all over South America. She had a consummate love for leading people to salvation.

Second, Arlene also was a prophetess. She was able to discern the voice of the Lord for situations and for people, and she would often call students or even pastors individually to give them a word from the Lord for their situation. The truth of the Word was proven time and time again as God confirmed the truth of his love and care to the hearts of the people.

Third, Arlene did not always have good health. There were times that she was sick and not feeling well, but she would drag herself to class because she did not want to miss her opportunity with the students. She persevered and paid a high price to serve the Lord, even while suffering. She was a great example of dedication, of perseverance in suffering, and of self-denial.

Fourth, Arlene Miller was a mother. She often stated in her classes or in missions conferences that she would like to have been married, but she was willing to give it up for the sake of the gospel. Single female missionaries have made great contributions in world missions, and she was a great example and champion of the challenge. Many students – both female and male alike – state how Arlene was a 'spiritual mother' to them! She was a mother to me and my family, as well as to Paul and Gabi Schmidgall in Germany, and to others.

Through her influence, she has children all over the world who are preaching the gospel. When her ministry in Israel ended, it seemed like she was at the end of the road and that God was finished with her. God, however, was opening the door for her to replicate herself through missionaries from Latin America. The result has been the multiplication of her ministry around the world through these disciples of Arlene Miller.

During the last years of her life, she suffered as she lay in a bed, confined to a nursing home. She often commented on how she just wanted to go home to be with the Lord. I truly believe that God gave her grace to endure until Marcia Anderson could come off the mission field to dedicate the time and effort to write Arlene's story. Arlene's life would not be complete without her leaving her testimony of God's grace and God's leading for the next generations of missionaries to learn from. Many, many thanks to Marcia for her time and dedication in this effort and especially for her vision to share Arlene's story for the glory of God.

John Thomas Hayes (MDiv, MA)
San Jose, California
September 30, 2019

Acknowledgements

When the LORD revealed to me that I was to return to America after 50 years of living in Iran, Fiji, the Philippines, Singapore, Israel, the Philippines (again), and Kenya, I knew it was to be a time to minister to my older sister who was in need of my help. I also knew, however, that my work as a missionary was not finished.

One day, two years prior to my 'retirement'[1] I had been visiting my sister, Miriam, in Cincinnati, Ohio. The thought occurred to me that I could visit Arlene Miller whom Janice McClung had informed me was in that very city. My sister took me to visit Arlene in her room at Meadowbrook Care Center. I didn't know Arlene very well, but I knew that she had given many years serving the Lord on the mission field – more than my 27 years as a missionary! I suggested to her that she should write her story. Later, I tried to send her a hand-recorder to document it for someone to write. She declined, saying she could no longer hold a microphone for such a task.

Several days after the decision had been made for me to leave Kenya, I was walking to the downtown area of Eldoret when an idea popped into my head like a light bulb: 'I can write Arlene's story. I'll be in the same city!' I phoned her to share the good news, to which she replied, 'Oh, many people have said they would do that, but no one has!' 'Well, if I say I'll do it, I will,' I rejoined.[2]

When I told Dr John Christopher Thomas[3] over lunch about the project I envisioned, I asked, 'How would I get someone to publish this?'

---

[1] Officially, I am still an associate missionary, able to teach in various places in the world as needed, representing Church of God World Missions, Cleveland, Tennessee. I was honored, however, as a retired missionary from the African 'field' at the General Assembly (July 31-August 3, 2018) convened in Orlando, Florida.

[2] At that time I had no idea that I was the answer to a very specific prayer of Janet Metzger (Douglas), who knew that Arlene had been reduced to 'idleness' by her disabilities and realized that this was very challenging for her. Janet prayed that Arlene would have something to do! This book was that 'something'. I certainly thought of it as 'something' I needed to do, but didn't realize how much Arlene needed that very same 'something!'

[3] Dr Thomas, the Clarence J. Abbott Professor of Biblical Studies at the Pentecostal Theological Seminary (then the Church of God School of Theology) in

He answered, 'CPT Press will do it! How long do you think it will take you?'

We had a publisher! Thank you, Drs. Thomas and Lee Roy Martin![4] I told them it would take two years. The writing took half that amount of time, primarily due to the urgency which Arlene felt to have it published, but of course editing must be done as well!

As I visited with long-time supporters of my ministry, Mark and Marcy Webb, I realized that visiting Arlene in Meadowbrook was going to cost me at least $50 a visit by Uber. They offered to continue to support me as a missionary with transportation money so that I could accomplish the task. Thank you, Mark and Marcy.

As work progressed, we realized that Arlene couldn't remember many details due to the morphine which moderated the pain for her. I realized I needed help. Thanks to Dr Robert Douglas and John Hayes who came to my aid by phone and email – John painstakingly translating all of the information about the students from the Missionary Training Center (MTM) from Portuguese to English. Thanks also goes to Janice McClung who helped me get in touch with people I needed to find to help with the effort.[5] Thanks to all those who read and critiqued the text: Janice and Grant McClung, Vicki Creel, Jamie Donaldson, Pat Weatherby, Fadi Rahayel, Becky Wayne – but most especially Martha Wong, a skilled copy-editor who has spent innumerable hours refining this document with a fine-tooth comb!

Special thanks to Jamie Donaldson and Dianne Bullock and Jo Egbert. These three helped form community for Arlene in her isolation and helped me substantially with the garnering of information

---

Cleveland, Tennessee, was my very first lecturer at that institution in 1988. I subsequently became his Student Assistant and later taught at his invitation at the seminary. Later still, I was tasked to write a commentary on 1 Samuel by Dr Lee Roy Martin and Dr Thomas for the Pentecostal Commentary Series. The Centre for Pentecostal Theology, which Dr Thomas directs, undertakes the publication of scholarly works at CPT Press in Cleveland and publishes in conjunction with Brill Publishing in the Netherlands.

[4] Dr Lee Roy Martin is Professor of Old Testament and Biblical Languages at the Pentecostal Theological Seminary, Old Testament Editor for the Pentecostal Commentary Series and Associate Director for the Centre for Pentecostal Studies.

[5] After Arlene's death many other people helped, including her sister, Phyllis. Thank you, Phyllis, for providing additional photos for this book. These photos are now part of the archives of the Pentecostal Research Center, Squires Library, Cleveland, Tennessee.

from Arlene. Thanks to Suhaila Khoury, who identified people on photos after Arlene had passed on.

I am deeply indebted to you all.

Arlene wanted to express her thanks to me for my patience – for all the hard work I'd done trying to pull her thoughts together! She also added her thanks also to Drs. Thomas and Martin for being willing to publish her life story. Yes, we are both grateful.

Annette, the director of nursing, was outstanding in her patience in trying to help Arlene during her confinement. There were too many wonderful aides to try to name them. Especially, thanks to Sylvia, who always tried her best to do things the way Arlene wanted.

Arlene was also grateful for weekly visits from Doris Cockerham and many others, especially those from King's Point Church of God.

1

CHOCOLATES AND MUSHROOMS

The first time I met Arlene, she and I (Marcia), were giving our testimonies at a Church of God World Missions gathering. Each of us was giving a short talk about what the Lord was doing where we were working. I'll never forget Arlene's story. It was her now 'famous' story about the chocolates. But let her tell it herself.

> I love Russell Stover dark chocolate-covered caramels. One time in Aboud, I really missed them, and I said to Margaret,[7] 'I'd just love to have some of those Russell Stover's dark chocolate-covered caramels'. It happened that it was one of those times when people came to tour Israel[8] in groups and a delegation was coming to visit us that very next day. To my surprise, one of the women asked to see me, specifically. I had never met her before. She said that she had been in a store looking at a display rack of chocolates before coming to Israel. 'The Lord told me to stop and buy one of those boxes and to bring it to Arlene Miller.'
>
> I said, 'I will tell you what kind of chocolates they are!' And I did, I knew exactly the kind they were because I recognized the shape of the box. The Lord reminded me that day that he wants his

---

[7] Margaret Gaines, missionary founder of the school in Aboud where Arlene taught and administered for 20 years.

[8] Arlene would often refer to Israel as 'Palestine,' the term used by the British in its governance of the territory. The name derives from the Philistines who were present in the nation of Israel in its formative years and now has been adopted by the Arabs living in Israel. To provide continuity I have used the United Nations mandated name for the country, which is Israel, throughout the book.

missionary daughters to know that nothing is impossible for him and that he delights in encouraging his children.

The day that I reminded Arlene of the chocolate story, she said,

To me, the story that was more a miracle is the one about morel mushrooms. Now, at missions conferences, I'm often asked to tell about great things God has done for us – miracles. I would respond by telling them that I was more interested in the little things that God has provided when he knows we have made sacrifices. It is one of the ways that God lets us know he cares for us on the mission field. Various people have remembered significant incidents in my life, but it seems to me that the thing that amazed me the most is one you haven't heard.

I quickly interjected, 'Morel mushrooms!'
'You mean you have heard about that one?'
'Yes, someone told me the story when I mentioned I was helping you write your story'.

And so, Arlene began to tell me her version of the morel mushroom story.

As far as I knew morel mushrooms did not grow in Israel and I've always wanted to contact the department of agriculture there for an explanation because of what happened that time. In the village I lived in, in the winter time especially, the people on the West Bank really struggled. Because they didn't have a lot of money, they would look for food wherever they could find it. By the time spring came they would walk as far as Jericho, looking for any sign of green, anything that grew on the trees or beneath them. I had just said to Margaret one spring day, 'Oh, I would love to be at home because this is mushroom season and the mushrooms only last about two weeks'. I walked out of the basement apartment. I had to go up five steps to get to ground level and what do you think I found?

There were mushrooms growing underneath a pine tree. I couldn't believe it. I went back into the house, grabbed a pan and went back outside to collect them. I had the sense to know that there is a mushroom that looks like the morel, but is very dangerous and poisonous. But, I picked those mushrooms anyway and Margaret said, 'I've never seen you so excited'.

I went to the school and got out the encyclopedia. We also called in a lot of the old Arab men of the village. These were shepherds who went out into the fields, looking for food. 'We've never seen anything like it', they said. And they begged me, 'Sister, don't eat those mushrooms. They will kill you. Please don't eat them.'

I laughed and said, 'At least I'll die happy'. Later I had friends in the U.S. Google them and they said those mushrooms normally grow under ash trees but not in that particular part of Israel. I knew it was just one of God's loving miracles.

2

MEADOWBROOK CARE CENTER

To begin my story, let me (Arlene) tell you why I am in the Meadowbrook Care Center in Cincinnati, Ohio. I have a bile duct problem. I've had seven painful operations on the bile duct where they actually cut and stretched the duct. You see, the bile in my body flows in reverse. Then, because of the vagus nerve I have this problem with passing out. It's not when I am full of tension but when I am under physical stress and pain the vagus nerve acts that way in response to the bile – it will make me pass out.

While home on leave in 2009, I had gone to see someone in town to have my hair done. When I stopped the car, I was one block off the US highway in the center of my hometown, Hillsboro, Ohio. The temperature outside was very hot and I could feel that I was going to pass out. I knew that with my remote control I could get the car door open and sit down where I would fall on something soft. But it was so hot in the car I was afraid I would pass out and die from the heat. You see, I had to put the key in the ignition to start the air conditioning and I knew I didn't have time to do that. So, instead, I started walking across the street when I collapsed and broke my neck as I fell on the curb.

Now I have twelve screws in my neck. It's not paralysis on my right side. It's severe nerve damage. But I can just barely move my right leg at all. My hand is clenched on the right side and frozen at the elbow all the way to my shoulder. They have told me that if I ever get one screw out of alignment, I will be a quadriplegic. That would be terrible because I couldn't use the telephone. I can use my left hand for that, but it doesn't have much feeling, either.

Lying in a hospital bed for all of these years has not been easy. However, God will still send people my way to minister to me and will also send people for me to minister to. The church people were so wonderful when I came here. When I first came into the nursing home nine years ago, I had to wear slacks for therapy. I've never worn slacks; I've always worn dresses or skirts; but therapy necessitated it. One lady from Kings Point Church of God in Ohio did the shopping. She went out and bought me Alfred Donner clothes and I looked so smart. Every day people would look to see what I had on! That went on until I couldn't get around anymore even with help and had to begin wearing hospital gowns all the time. I miss those smart clothes!

I've never asked God, 'Why?' My grandmother was my first pastor in Ohio and she always taught us, 'Don't question God, he knows what he is doing. He usually doesn't answer that 'Why?' question anyway. I'm not distressed. I'm not discouraged. But, I said that the Enemy of my soul is out to destroy me.

When I first came to Meadowbrook, with two aides helping me, I could walk a few steps with the walker and if aides put me in the wheelchair I could go from room to room, visiting others. But my body started getting worse: my one foot was becoming drawn over to the side, my hand was becoming clenched more and I couldn't bend from the waist down. After that they couldn't put me into the wheelchair anymore.

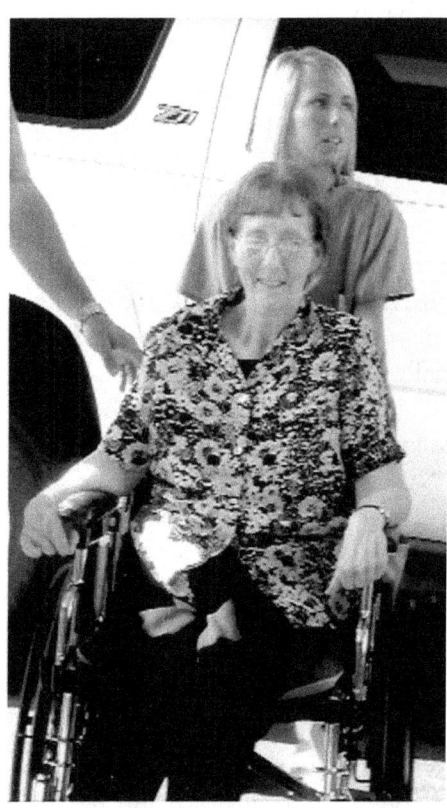

Arlene and helper from Meadowbrook Care Center as she prepares to speak at a Missions Conference in Kings Point, Ohio, in 2010

Especially this last year, it's been so difficult; it's as if God has said to the devil, 'Have you considered my servant Job?' Remember the story? Satan said, 'But You've got a wall of protection around him. Remove the wall and You'll see what he (she) will do'.

Now, I'm no Job by any means, but sometimes I feel that way. Sometimes the aide situation is bad. Some of them can be so mean and so cruel, but others come in and give me a hug. Some come in when they are not even my aide and give me a kiss and tell me good morning. One always brings me my meal even though she's not my aide. I've had many good aides. For example, Sylvia. She is a favorite of mine because she takes time to do things just right. Patty is also a favorite. Antonia and several others. It is easier because they know what they are doing, and I do not have to worry about it. Eileen is one of our best nurses. I especially would like to thank Annette, our director of nursing. She is especially patient with me and goes out of her way to get me aides that she knows are able to take care of me.

But then, there is the pain. Now, I must tell you, they are giving me morphine. My arm hurts from my shoulder down and I hate taking that drug, but sometimes it is just necessary.

There have been disappointments, too. I really enjoy being able to help others, but one person I was witnessing to has been transferred to another unit and I miss being able to help him; however, I have been able to minister to people here.

Just last night I had a distressing encounter with one of the nurses who had become as frustrated with me over the detailed needs of an incapacitated person who needs pillows put 'just so' and has to be diapered and cared for like a baby. After venting her annoyance with all of my demands, she came back into the room, apologized for her lack of patience and said that she needed me to help her. She subsequently rolled in an old man, a Christian, who was facing death. He was feeling very alone and really wanted to die. I said, 'Join the club. I've prayed to die, too, but God has not said "yes" to that prayer yet'. He laughed at that. I felt such compassion for the old man and was able to hold his hand, pray for him and minister hope. When we prayed, I told him that God knows best and that he will take us in his time and there has to be a reason why we are still here. That man often stops by to see me.

I am 'down' but definitely not 'out'.

God still speaks to me vividly for some people. The Spirit was telling me some things about what one worker at Meadowbrook was going through. His feelings became mine. I don't like talking about it because it sounds so egotistical, and I know I'm nothing in the eyes of the Lord, just a grain of sand. But, when the Lord lays someone on my heart, I actually physically feel what the person is going through and sense in my spirit exactly what people are experiencing.

That person here at the Care center was really in distress. I was awakened at two o'clock in the morning and felt like I couldn't breathe. There was an awful heaviness in my chest. In fact, I thought I would smother to death. That's when the Spirit spoke to me and said, 'That is the way (a certain nurse) is feeling'. Because I knew immediately it was what this particular nurse was going through, later that morning I called him in. I told him, 'Kneel down because I want to get ahold of your hand and talk to you for just a minute. I was awakened about two this morning. You were going through the most awful grief and pain.' Then I reached over and touched his chest and said, 'You could hardly breathe'.

He said, 'That's right', and I prayed for him right then and there.

After that, I ministered to this same young man many times and saw the Lord deal with him in an interesting way. The Lord showed me how to minister to Him. He showed me that I could use the words of some of the old hymns. Now this young man had just begun to attend a church that sang a lot of the old hymns that I was familiar with, but he didn't know any of them well. I would have the woman in the social service office look up the hymns and type them out for me. Then I would ask that man to come into my room. Some of the words of the hymns that encouraged him were, 1) 'All the way my Savior leads me. What have I to ask beside?' 2) 'Rescuing the perishing, Care for the dying. Touched by a loving hand, wakened by kindness, cords that are broken will vibrate once more.'

That last song really touched him. I said, 'I see your heart, not with the heart strings broken on both ends; they are still attached on one end and they will be attached again. "Cords that were broken will vibrate once more."' Hymns like those ministered to him. When I gave him the words to those songs, he was always encouraged. He said, 'Every time we talk it helps me'.

I will give you some more examples in which I've been able to minister to people in the Center. One time I was in my wheelchair out in the hallway. A man came down the hallway to visit his mother. He stopped in front of me. I'd never seen him before in my life. 'You', he said.

'Me, what?'

'You are the one to go talk to my mother'.

'Well, what makes you think I'm the one to go talk to your mother?' I didn't even know who his mother was.

He said, 'That's what the Lord told me when I saw you'.

Now, I have to be very careful. I know being a chaplain is an extremely difficult thing; I've talked to several chaplains about this issue and I've been through a chaplaincy course myself. One has to be sure she is not doing something a family member would object to.

The man continued, 'My mother is dying and she's very afraid and she doesn't know if she's ready to go or not'.

Well, I asked further, 'What about your family? Do you have any brothers and sisters?'

'Yes, I have a sister'.

'Would she object to my talking to your mother?

'No.'

I asked about his mother's religious background. You see, I like to know where they are coming from. I wanted to know what terminology to use. For example, if I knew he was Pentecostal, I would talk in one way, but if he was Catholic I might use different words. She was from a mainline denomination. By her son's answers, I knew she would understand me, so I went in and talked to her. I asked her if she knew Jesus. She replied that she did. I reminded her that perfect love casts out fear and that she didn't need to be afraid of the life to come. We prayed and I said, 'Now do you understand? Are you going to be afraid?'

'No. I'm not going to be afraid anymore.'

I went back a little bit later that evening and she was smiling. 'Are you ok?'

'Yes.'

That same night she passed away.

Now aides are not allowed to tell us when someone is dying, but several times they would come and say, 'You need to go see Mary', and I knew that meant she was dying and I needed to go see her. God cares.

3

GETTING STARTED

How did I get to Aboud? How did I become a missionary, anyhow?[9] I was born on June 8, 1940, at my grandmother's home near a town in Highland County, Ohio, to Frank Oliver Miller and Mary Frances (Reed) Miller. I am the oldest of four sisters.[10] We lived in Hillsboro in a rented house until I was about five when we moved to a 4-acre plot of ground two miles outside of Hillsboro. Normally, we had one cow and one time we even had a pig! I've always been grateful for those simple beginnings because it helped me adjust later to village life in Israel.

Born Again

Mother and Father were both teachers in the church and my father was the clerk for the Church of God in Carmel, Ohio, for forty years. I got saved at twelve in a revival with Reverend Everette Bragg at the little country church where my grandmother pastored. When Rev. Bragg came for that revival, I just knew it was my time to be born-again, and I began to pray while we were still standing. In my prayer I said, 'If Frances Caddell comes back to me and invites me to the altar, I'll know for sure it's my time'. I was too embarrassed to go forward alone and there weren't any other children at the altar. Frances was a young woman who mothered us young people though

---

[9] Arlene was a credentialed minister in the Church of God, Cleveland, Tennessee, holding a licensed-ordained certificate.

[10] One sister, Phyllis had power of attorney for her, wrote her newsletter for her and did her banking.

she had no children of her own at that time. The Lord answered my prayer. Frances came to me. When we went together to the altar, I felt so happy, so full of joy, because I knew my sins had been forgiven.

Sisters (L-R) Nadine, Elaine, Phyllis, Arlene. Parents (seated), Frank Oliver Miller and Mary Frances (Reed) Miller.

Before that, we had attended services at a church near Carmel which had sawdust on the floor and kerosene lanterns to light the sanctuary. The sawdust and the timber to build that church came from the mill that my paternal grandfather had operated on this property. He had allowed them to build this church that my maternal grandmother pastored, called the Old Tabernacle.

The next church we worshipped in was 17 miles away. We rented an Odd Fellow's Lodge Hall in a town called Sinking Springs.

Finally, we moved back to a property that the church had purchased in Carmel. My father had drawn up the plans for the church that was built on the church's own property, not my grandparents', but in the same community where the first church with sawdust-covered floor stood. This church was constructed of white cement block and had a wonderful bell tower. I remember that my father rang the bell of that church long and loud every Sunday. All of the churches in our little community had bells and I loved to hear them ring.

Going to church was important to me and I treasured Scripture. What did we memorize? Of course, the easiest Bible verse was Jn 11.35, 'Jesus wept'. I was a pretty normal kid who often recited that one! Psalm 37.27, 'The steps of a good man are ordered by the Lord, he delights in his way'. Proverbs 3.6, 'In all your ways acknowledge him and he will direct your path'. As years passed by, I think Psalms 23 and 51 became my most cherished Psalms.

Filled with The Spirit

When I was in high school, I wanted to receive the baptism of the Holy Spirit and therefore I knew I needed to be sanctified. In our church we learn that the Holy Spirit can only fill a clean vessel and he looks for a totally surrendered heart. I felt the need to be out of sight of people because it was so personal. Of course, I knew you could be get sanctified in a church, but I needed to be in the woods. We lived at the edge of a subdivision where I could easily go into the woods right by the house. When I was sure I was alone, I knelt down on the ground and fell on my face. When I arose from that precious time of surrender, I felt such a joyous cleansing. I knew God could now baptize me with his Spirit.

I always knew from the time I got saved that I would become a missionary. You might wonder why? As I've told you before, I was saved when I was about 12, but my desire to become a missionary grew, especially after I received the Holy Ghost, whom I received at the altar at church when I was about 17. Many people talk about tarrying to receive the Holy Spirit, but with me there was no struggle. I just went to the altar, asked him to fill me with his Spirit and he did! I began to pray in other tongues and as I've told you, God gave me a spirit of discernment. The other young people were amazed because they knew what a detailed person I was. I guess they thought receiving the Baptism of the Holy Spirit would be a complicated thing for me, but it wasn't. He just came when I invited him to come! I knew I was part of God's big family on earth.

Family Gatherings

We were one big happy family, too, especially because four in father's family had married four in mother's family. That meant many of us were double cousins, so we were really one big extended bunch! Like every other close family, we enjoyed being together. Many of us attended the same church, but all of us definitely gathered for family gatherings every holiday: Christmas, New Year's Eve, Easter, and Thanksgiving. Usually our reunions were at our grandparents' house. Everyone brought food – everything you could imagine. There were beef and noodles and chicken and noodles, and other less traditional food like tacos. My Aunt Marjorie had lived in Arizona for a year and learned to make tacos, so she would bring those on New Year's Eve.

I always enjoyed time with my cousins, riding sleds, just having fun times being together. Several were my own age or around my age because most families had three or four children. Music was very important: one aunt played the guitar, an uncle played the mandolin and an aunt played the banjo.

In summer we would get together at the State Hill Park for a reunion and some acquaintances in the community were there, too. These were country people who came from as far away as seventeen miles. Together they would play music and everyone would sing Southern Gospel Music and old 'folk songs' like the 'Red River Valley'. On the Fourth of July we would always go to Fort Hill where there was an old earthen fort and a big stone and timber shelter house especially prepared for people who were having picnics. It had been an old Shawnee Indian stomping ground and was a very pleasant place to have a picnic and see fireworks. The people who gathered were from different churches so that helped me have a little broader perspective on life, too.

Special to me was Cousin Eleanor. We were among the older cousins, so we often paired up. There were some cousins two or three years younger that my sisters would also gang up with. One of the crazy, fun things we did was to have eating contests with Aunt Martha's beef and noodles or Aunt Dorothy's chicken and noodles. I can still taste that great food! Later I would discover that food is an important part of every strong community in the world.

My grandmother impacted me spiritually. She was my greatest mentor. Some people have said about me, 'Arlene was never young until she was old'. I would go home with my grandmother on Sunday's after church. Imagine, as as a 14-year-old, she would discuss church problems with me and we would pray about them – things she should have been able to discuss with other people, I guess, but could not. I learned she was a very lonely person. I think God wanted me to see how she felt because I was going to have to be lonely lots of times myself. I saw how she had the resilience to walk through that lonely place. Later, when I would experience many lonely times, I didn't have anyone to listen like my grandmother had, but I remembered her.

I'm amazed how much grandmother trusted me. I know she believed that there was a call on my life. At one church service my uncle, who was also my pastor, stood with his eyes closed as we were standing at the altar. Suddenly he walked over and put his hands on my head and said, 'Mom's mantle has fallen on you'. I knew I was going to be a missionary; so it didn't really surprise me, but it surely encouraged me.

Like my grandmother, I loved to read. I read *Gone with the Wind* in two days and made the librarian so mad that when I brought it back, she said, 'There is a list of people waiting for this book and you took it and didn't even read it!'

'I did read it!' She couldn't believe I read it so fast.

My love for reading surely came from my grandmother. She could read a 500-page book in two days and I could, too. I love to read. I used to read lots of books on my Kindle here in the nursing home until I couldn't hold it any longer. I especially liked the Christmas gatherings. Though Aunt Marjorie was only about the age of the older cousins, she could really make that piano sing and we would gather around the piano and belt out Christmas songs like, 'Up on the Housetop', and all the other popular tunes. By the way, we were proud of Marjorie because she also played at the Methodist church.

We drew names at Thanksgiving time for the Christmas exchange gift time. My Grandfather Miller would give each grandchild a silver fifty-cent piece. We could buy quite a lot with fifty cents, but he expected that we would save it. My grandparents were careful to give each grandchild the same to be fair and there were quite a lot of grandchildren by that time.

Elementary School

I attended a two-story, red brick elementary school (grades 1-6) in Hillsboro, the county seat of Highland County, which was two miles away from our home. After I finished grade six, I attended a big, beautiful, red-brick junior high and high school. I remember especially the distinctive white pillars at the front. The elementary schools were at both ends of town with the high school in the middle.

I always liked Social Studies classes because, even then, I wanted to travel. Like many other people who prefer the social sciences, I suppose, I disliked math very much. I was interested especially in Europe – Switzerland, Germany, and England. Old romantic castles and ruins engaged my imagination. I was also fascinated by Holland with its dikes and wooden shoes. My always-supportive mother would make construction paper models of the houses and things we studied in Social Studies class to help us learn. My love of social studies as a child made me more open to people of other cultures – in fact, I've always been fascinated by people of those cultures, and that helped me adjust as a missionary. My fourth-grade teacher gave me a love for geography, and the principal, who loved history, encouraged me in my love for history and traveling.

High School

I always loved school, though I hated math and science. Because I liked school so much, I always wanted to be a teacher. I graduated from Hillsboro High School on May 29, 1958. When I went to college, I found out how excellent our teachers were, who gave us a good foundation. I corresponded with Miss Treadwell, the English teacher at Hillsboro High School, for years and even went to see her one day, years later. She was so special to me: her interest in English literature intrigued me; she could make it come alive, especially the poems. Even when I went to Israel, she kept in touch. Later she retired and moved back to her hometown across the state, but she wrote to me and told me what she was doing. I felt like she was a friend.

We also had some very good teachers at church when we were growing up, too – my aunt and my mother.

At church, we had a quintet – four girls and one boy – with whom I sang ordinary hymns accompanied by my cousin on the piano. It was a good environment for my faith to grow.

Friends

One of my special neighbor friends was Janet Stultz who lived near us. It seems all the other church people lived ten miles in every direction from the church so we didn't have our own vacation bible school, but I would go with Janet to the Nazarene Church's Vacation Bible School in Hillsboro. When we were in elementary school, we started the Playmate Club together. She and I and other neighbor kids subscribed to Playmate magazine which had stories, puzzles, and the names of children who wanted pen pals to write to. We both had pen pals and enjoyed that. Janet had a playhouse, too, that we girls had our meetings in. Of course, we played some 'boy' games, too, like cops and robbers with our cap guns, etc. Janet and I were friends from first grade to college. Later we both went to Morehead State College and both ended up being teachers – she in our hometown, and I in Batavia, Ohio.

I was disappointed that Janet and I wouldn't be roommates in college, but it wasn't as horrible as I thought it would be. God was helping me. As a young Pentecostal I couldn't go to movies and other 'worldly' activities. It hurt very much that Janet and I chose different pathways because we had been best friends all through grade school. It is not easy being Pentecostal, especially when you are young and, especially, in those days. Women didn't wear slacks or shorts, we had long hair, and didn't go swimming in public places. My hair was hanging down to my waist, so I definitely looked distinctive. I was doing that sacrificially to honor the Lord and I knew it was important to go on about what God wanted me to do. I had a drive in me to do God's will. If I hadn't already received a clear call from God, I might have gone a different direction myself.

Sometimes missionaries came and stayed in our home. One that especially encouraged me in missions was Everett Bragg who had been a missionary to Barbados and the Virgin Islands. I thought the Lord would send me to Cuba where the Spanish would be easy to learn! My idea of a missionary was to be an evangelist. In my mind, missionaries were preachers. After all, they were supposed to go and make disciples and plant churches, right? Yet, I wanted to be a teacher. I didn't understand this. It didn't fit together in my mind. I knew the Lord was telling me to be a missionary, but he was also telling me to be an elementary teacher! Later I was to discover I could do both and this was wonderful for me. Furthermore, the Lord had impressed on me when I was about 15 or 16, that I was not to date any one person too long and fall in love with them, because I was not going to have time for it in the work he had for me to do. Actually, we usually did things in groups anyway, like attending basketball and football games, so that wasn't difficult for me.

I remember one of the first sermons that I preached at Youth Camp. It was wonderful to see the youth respond. After I preached that time, a pastor came and talked to me. He said, 'After you've preached a few years, you'll be able to take those scripture verses and cut them down to two or three!'

I think at heart, I'm really a preacher. I get straight to the point. I don't mince words. What is the main message that I want people to receive when I preach? Salvation is first and foremost. I also preach a lot on sanctification because there's not much sanctification mentioned any more. It is cleansing and a definite work of grace. How did I know what to preach? I always liked to preach about characters in the Bible. I would pray; and as I read the Bible, I would just know what to preach.

How do I hear God? I think the Word teaches us that if it can't be backed up by the Word don't believe it. When God has me speak a word to someone, I often see a vision, and he usually speaks to me through the Word. Hymns also speak to me. On many occasions the LORD will bring a line of the song that speaks into my situation, often one of Fanny Crosby's songs.

Discerning things in the Spirit is not a new gift. I've had it since I was young. When I was about eighteen, I told a woman evangelist after she finished preaching that I had discerned something as she spoke. The Lord showed me that she felt abandoned by her husband. It seems her husband was not a believer and she was having a hard time about that. She responded, 'How old are you? I can't believe you saw that.' I'm so grateful God cares about all of the things that affect our lives, even the little ones that don't seem worth mentioning to anyone.

Another person who greatly influenced me in my early life was evangelist Ruth Steele. I was about 18 when I met her. She lived in Dayton, Ohio. Evangelists in our church would hold special evening services, usually for a week, that we called revivals. These were times when people were encouraged to draw closer to God and strengthen their spiritual lives. Ruth held revivals in many places, even in my little country church in Carmel. We rented a little house for her to stay in when she came for the five weeks of revival. One time I wanted to give Ruth an offering, personally. Do you know that without opening the envelope she could tell me what denominations the bills were in that envelope? When she saw my amazement, she told me that the Lord wanted me to know that he still does things like that in this day and time. She had discernment like you wouldn't believe. As we sat together in a car outside the church one evening, she told me that she had seen the people in our church before she came and even where they were sitting. I was really in awe of her. I already knew I was going to be a minister and she really encouraged me in that.

One time when I was in high school, I got really dizzy – horribly dizzy – and they didn't know what was wrong with me. I called Ruth Steele and told her they were taking me to the hospital in Columbus. She said, 'They won't find anything wrong with you'. And they didn't.

Time for College
I went to college in 1958 and studied for two years at Morehead State, which is a university now, in Morehead, Kentucky. I studied elementary education with a minor in history. Later, in the summers of 1961 and 1962, I also took some courses at Miami University in Oxford, Ohio, and Cumberland College in Williamsburg, Kentucky. During that first year in college, I had been attending a little Church of God outside the town of Morehead in a place called Farmers. The minister, Brother Flannery, had just finished his sermon and was saying, 'Let's stand and dismiss in prayer'. From the time he said that, before he even opened his mouth to pray, I had a vision. I saw a woman. I saw her hair. I saw her cheekbones. I would have recognized her anywhere if I ever saw her again. The Holy Spirit had said, 'She is a missionary'. I knew she was single, and I knew she needed help right then. She was kneeling outside on very stony ground. And so, I said, 'Brother Flannery, I have to tell you something, because we need to pray'. I started telling the congregation what I had seen. The whole church began weeping and they prayed for the young woman. The Spirit was 'bearing witness' that what I had seen was from the Lord.

Now, remember, we attended that little country church ten miles from Hillsboro. We were pretty remote – for example, we never got to go to youth camp. We didn't have too many officials visit our church, either; and I needed to find out who the person in the vision had been. I asked Ruth Steele because she traveled and evangelized a lot and knew lots of people in the church. 'Arlene, it has to be Margaret Gaines', she said. 'She's the only single woman we have on the field at this time.' I was fascinated by who this young woman was who had pioneered a work in Tunisia in those early years. I started reading everything Margaret had written.

Some people have commented, 'Everything about your life is so definite. You knew exactly.' I was very fortunate that way. It's true, I didn't have to pray and pray and pray. Of course, I did pray over every decision, but still I usually knew exactly what the Lord wanted me to do.

In college I had two to four roommates. I felt different in college, too, as a Pentecostal. My roommates didn't understand it, but fortunately we could talk about our faith and had many good conversations about it.

Because of finances, I had to stop college after two years and went to Batavia to teach for three years from 1960 to 1963. While I was teaching in Batavia, I met Sybil Cannon, who was a well-known state evangelist in North Carolina, Tennessee, and Ohio.

Sybil came to hold a revival in Batavia. The doctor told Sybil she needed someone to preach half time for her because she had a heart problem. At that time the Lord had been impressing on me that I needed to stop teaching school and get into church work. And so, when I told her I was called to preach, she said, 'Would you like to travel with me?' I gladly agreed. In our church, evangelists were itinerant preachers who went from church to church holding revivals like I talked about earlier. Sybil and I evangelized together for three years, and I also became a state evangelist in Tennessee. I have never had the problem of being unknown and unable to get started because the Lord has put me with people who were very well-known. When we traveled together, Sybil and I would overlap. While she would close one revival, I would start another set of meetings. And then she would join me or vice versa.[11] She influenced me greatly. She did not have much education. Sybil was mainly self-taught, but she could preach like a house-on-fire. She taught at youth camp, and like me, she was a 'character' preacher. I remember her especially preaching about Adam and stressing the question God gave to Adam 'Where are you?' I loved both teaching and preaching. After Sybil died, I used

---

[11] Sybil later lived with Arlene until her untimely death at the young age of 49.

a lot of her sermons because she was an excellent preacher who loved to preach on Elijah, Elisha, Job, Paul, and others.

Margaret Gaines

When the Six-day War came to Israel in 1967, I wrote to Margaret Gaines and said, 'I want you to know that God has put you on the heart of people who don't even know you but are praying for you'. I told her what had happened and what I had seen way back in 1958 in Batavia. She didn't respond to that letter.

Back to Morehead

After my years of evangelizing, I went back to Morehead and finished my Bachelor of Arts degree in August 1, 1968. I remember one time in World History class, that the professor was excellent on the New Testament, although it wasn't a Bible school. He would go all around the class and ask a question. 'Mr. So-and-So, what is the answer?' 'Miss So-and-So, what is the answer?' Finally, he would say, 'Miss Miller, please tell them'. He knew I had good Bible training. When my sister went to Lee University, they asked her what Bible school she had attended. They were surprised at her level of knowledge of the Bible, too. She was taking elementary education courses and took a few Bible courses, in which she excelled. Our home church was a little country church that averaged about 60 people on Sunday mornings, but we really had good teachers.

Teaching at Piqua

After graduating, I went back to teaching at Piqua for five years. I loved teaching reading because I used the old-fashioned phonics method. The principal in that school came and asked me how I learned to teach like that, because for the first time his daughter passed her fifth grade English exam. She had a learning disability and phonics really helped her.

I was still preaching at the state convention or teaching classes at those big conventions, which they would invite me to come and teach. During that period, I was occasionally the State Junior Youth Camp speaker.

Working on a Master's Degree

As I was teaching at Piqua, I began going back to school full time for my master's degree. The Lord had been impressing on me that I needed to get an advanced degree in elementary education. 'I'm going to be a missionary and you want me to work on a master's in elementary education?' To me, those things didn't fit together. Remember, I thought being a missionary meant I was to be an evangelist – a preacher, someone who planted churches – not a teacher. I guess I had forgotten something very, very important that my grandmother had taught me when I first went to Morehead college, 'Don't ask God, "Why?"' But I obeyed. I began working on my master's in elementary education at Wright State University in Dayton, Ohio. I was commuting from Piqua for my classes.

Meeting Margaret Gaines

In 1972, when Margaret was home on furlough, I met her for the first time at our church's General Assembly.[12] When she showed me pictures of the Arab school, the Holy Spirit spoke to me, 'You will be with her at this time next year. Get ready to let your board of education know.' I did not tell her what God had said to me because the whole world wanted to work with Margaret, and she had already had some who had come to Aboud, and they didn't last any time.

I wasn't the only one that thought Margaret and I belonged together in ministry. For example, Kash and Mary Lou Amburgy brought tourists to Israel about five times a year.[13] Mary Lou was someone who knew both Margaret and me. She had traveled to Israel and had been telling Margaret about me.

She would say, 'Arlene's a teacher. She could help you out here. She's also an evangelist. You do need someone to help you.' So, it was through Mary Lou that Margaret began to know about me. (At that time, I didn't know that Margaret Gaines hadn't even started her

---

[12] The General Assembly was a time when thousands of people gathered from all over the world to make decisions related to the church. At that time most missionaries would try to attend.

[13] They often brought materials we needed. One time they brought a gunny sack full of duplicating paper and they would usually ask Church of God people to donate batteries for us. They ran a Bargain Barn in Lebanon and often had displays at the State Convention of the Church of God in Chitaqua.

college education and had no training whatsoever in elementary education. I was so happy to find out that the Lord really knew what he was doing, training me both in evangelism and education. See, the Lord does all things well!)

In the spring of 1973, I got down on my knees one weekend and was praying, crying. 'God, I need to be fair to my board of education. I need to let them know about my plans for next year. I need to hear from Margaret if she wants me to help her, because I will not just walk out on this board of education at the last minute, leaving them to have to find someone else.' I finally sat down by my bed and continued crying and praying in the spirit (praying in tongues). 'No, listen to me,' I pleaded, 'I am telling you what is in my heart. I don't want to speak in tongues. I want to pray with understanding and tell you something.' I stopped three times until finally I gave in and prayed in the Spirit again. You see, the letter was already in the air. It came about three days later. The Lord heard that desperate prayer.

Margaret wrote to me and asked if I would come to help her in Aboud. I wrote back and told her, 'Yes', but I did not hear back from her. I wrote back again and told her my flight number and everything and still never heard from her. My father was very concerned and said, 'You're going to go, and you haven't heard from her?' But the Holy Spirit had told me to go, so I was going to go. The superintendent begged me to stay. The principal called the superintendent to ask the superintendent to talk me into not leaving. When the superintendent talked to me, he said, 'You are going to go whether we give you a leave of absence or not, aren't you?' He gave me a leave of absence. The teachers were shocked because they knew the school didn't give leaves of absence.

The Enemy didn't like my going on the mission field and would have liked to kill me. One day before I left, as my family and I watched from their home, a tornado lifted a tree straight up, right beside their home. Later, I was going out of my trailer, running to get ready to go to camp meeting. I fell, my legs flying out from under me on our dew-covered wooden deck. I could easily have broken every bone of my body. I hit my head and my hip had a big purple bruise for a long time.

Another time, on I-75 a car or truck swerved right in front of us. I hit my brakes. The last two things from my apartment were in the back of the car. An ironing board in the back of the car came flying to hit me in the back of my head leaving a purple lump and giving me a slight concussion. But I was determined to go, so I told my father that even if I couldn't walk, to just put a sign around my neck with my destination written on it and send me off. Satan can't prevent us unless God permits it. The Enemy had spoken to me and told me, 'I told you I would kill you if you went', but I've always known my life was in God's hands.

Bassem and Marlene, Hilda and Atallah, Gabi Schmidgall, Arlene, Paul Schmidgall, and Margaret Gaines, overlooking Jerusalem.

In the Church of God, missionaries are interviewed by the World Missions Board before they are assigned oversees, but I didn't have a World Missions appointment. Margaret asked for me to be approved because she needed help; but at that time, they didn't send single women at all, so I just went as a volunteer.[14] Incidentally, Margaret had to wait years before the Church of God recognized her work. Would she be there at the airport to meet me?

---

[14] After one year the church gave me $50 a month and a few others sent money to help. Eventually my support was raised to $150 and I was reimbursed for travel.

4

THE WEST BANK VILLAGE OF ABOUD

It was early in the summer of 1973[15] when I arrived at the airport in Tel Aviv. I don't remember the date, but I know it had to be after I finished the school year. I was greeted by a blast of hot, dry air. Would Margaret be at the airport? I looked around eagerly. Even though I'd not heard from her, I just knew she would be there! Not only was Margaret there, but also Walter and Elfriede Greiner from Germany. This overseer couple of the Church of God in the Middle East lived in Jerusalem at that time and graciously brought Margaret to meet me.[16] When Margaret told Pastor Greiner that she wasn't sure I would even be there because she never answered me, he nearly 'croaked!' When Margaret met me, she said, 'I was so busy'. That's all.

A Thousand Years Back in Time

Was I surprised by what I saw when we arrived in Tel Aviv? No, not really, because I had seen many movies, etc., of the Middle East. Remember, I was a geography teacher in elementary school, also, so I knew what to expect. But when I saw Aboud, I felt like I had been sent back a thousand years in time. For example, there were houses

---

[15] I finished my Master of Education degree at Wright State on June 10, 1973.

[16] Greiner loved Israel and was the one who was responsible for building the second and third floors of the parsonage of the church in Jerusalem. They had a yellow tag on their car, indicating they lived in the Israeli sector, so they could go freely to the airport. Margaret, living on what is now called the West Bank, had a blue tag and was limited where she could go.

still present in Aboud like those they find when they excavate archeological tells, where layer after layer had been built on top of each other. For example, there were still rounded-dome houses from the Ottoman Empire time. There were goats, camels, men and women with long robes and head dresses, palm trees, and olive trees. There was no electricity and there were no telephones.

Government

Aboud is not really very far from Tel Aviv (probably about fifty miles). In fact, if it is a very clear day when you stand on the hillside in Aboud you can actually see the Mediterranean Sea, beside which Tel Aviv sits. At that time the Israelis called Aboud, 'Occupied Territory', and there was no Palestinian Authority yet. We were under both Israeli military administration and Jordanian civil administration.[17] If people in Aboud wanted to travel or come to the States, they had to have Jordanian passports. Like today, it was a difficult time because of the animosity between Jew and Arab.

Transportation

What would you see in Aboud in 1973? The town of Aboud had no post office – nothing. We didn't even have a mailbox. Instead, we went to Jerusalem once a week for our mail. The Arabs went to Ramallah for theirs. There were no supermarkets in our village, only Israeli ones in Jerusalem. For 3000 people in our village there were only 2 cars. Besides our bus, the Catholic priest also had a vehicle. Now, Margaret and I had just one car for years: a blue Volkswagen bus. My last two years there I was given a beige Volkswagen Jetta. When my friend came to visit me from the States, she said, 'I can't believe it. You are pale, the house is beige, the desert land is beige, and you get a beige car!' Later a few of the people in the village also got cars and a few got taxis.

Before there were taxis, a bus would come once in the morning at 5 or 6 o'clock and return about 3 pm in the afternoon to take people

---

[17] Jordan annexed the 'West Bank' after the 1948 Arab-Israeli conflict. They made Ramallah the administrative capitol, though technically, they considered Jerusalem the capitol. In the 1967 War the Israelis took control of this area. The Palestinian Authority was created following the 'Oslo Accords' in 1993.

back and forth to work. If someone died, we had to use my car to take them to the morgue. The nearest hospital was half an hour away, so if someone was going to have a baby, we also used my car to take them. One woman almost gave birth in the car. I turned around and looked in the back seat and saw that she was standing because the baby was coming, so I quickly took her back to the house and she gave birth on the veranda. Otherwise she would have had that baby in the back seat! Years before, a doctor in Tunis had told Margaret she needed to learn how to deliver babies, but I never delivered one, though it was a close call!

At Home in Aboud

We lived in one of the nicest houses in the village, which was a two-story, hand-carved stone house with a half apartment underneath.

Arlene and Margaret at home.

We had a tiny, little kitchen, a combined dining room and living room plus Margaret's bedroom on the ground floor. At first, we stayed together, but Margaret always got up at 5 a.m. to pray and study and I'm a late riser; so she arranged for me to have a bedroom on the second floor. She had rented the house from an old man, Abu

Khalil, his wife Um Khahil,[18] and daughter Muneera, who worked in Ramallah. The wife, especially, was so kind. She even took care of me when I was sick.

I had to go outside to go up to my room on the second floor. Because of stone-throwing I had to be upstairs before dark. When the Jewish settlers came by, going outside was not safe because youths would throw stones at the Israeli soldiers who would then in return shoot tear gas at those young men. That tear gas was lethal. It caused people with breathing problems to die and pregnant women to miscarry. People would have to run and close the windows very quickly. In our village it didn't happen often, but in Jerusalem it often did. One time I saw soldiers tell people to get off the street because they were preparing to use tear gas; then before the people could respond, I saw the soldiers ready to release the gas. I cried out, 'Don't you dare do that! Give them time to get into their houses!'

Margaret did the cooking and I did the dishes. Because my upstairs room was without a bathroom, unfortunately, I needed to use the bathroom in the landlord's part of the house. Sometimes the family members were there when I needed to use it. It was a real nuisance, but I managed.

I had a large room to myself (perhaps 12 x 12 feet) with an ample desk, specially made for me by a carpenter in Bierzeit Ridhhu, where I could prepare my lessons. Biereit's little tiny shop housed only one little carpenter. He made everything for the school and our house. We would draw what we wanted, and he would make it exactly like we specified. He couldn't believe we wanted cupboards behind every door. I drew a cabinet that went almost to the ceiling. It had drawers in it so that where I sat on my bed, I could reach two shelves and set my coffee cup on one. He was amazed at the things we drew for him to make. But he made every item that we asked for. Margaret and I both had deep, beautiful desks. The room had a veranda until later Margaret surprised me and turned it into a bathroom.

Though I know some people go up on the roof tops at certain times of the day when a breeze comes from the Mediterranean, the only time I went up on the roof was to check on the solar heating panels. It was usually hot up there, but the veranda in the front of the house was a nice place to cool off. Fans also helped us cool off.

---

[18] *Abu* means father, *Um* means mother in Arabic.

The houses were stone and had high ceilings which also made the houses cooler.

Many things about our lives were quite ordinary. For example, we didn't dress like the Arabs, just dressed in clothing like we would in America.

Food

A general store stood in front of our house that had basic things like soap, pop (soda), grain, etc. Arabs made their bread at home in a big hole in the ground lined with small stones. After the stones were heated, the bread *khubz taboon* was cooked on those stones. Every home had a different type oven above ground for the *pita* bread. The bread would bake, lining the bottom of that oven. We had a regular convection oven in the kitchen, but no oven in the ground, so other people in the village would often give us bread. It's a hard job to bake bread that way for only two people. I think the neighbors would have always provided our bread, but sometimes we enjoyed a change and would buy French-style baguettes in Jerusalem.

We enjoyed *hummus* (made from ground chickpeas), salad, and similar things. In the first years we bought these in the supermarket in Jerusalem, but later we could buy them at the little shop in front of our house. The Jerusalem supermarket also sold those French baguettes which we enjoyed, served with tangy white feta cheese made from goat's milk. We, however, ate mainly American food – chicken and dumplings, etc. The Arabs loved the sage dressing we made for American thanksgiving. And yes, we even had turkey stuffed with cornbread dressing flavored with sage. They loved it. Arabs were familiar with sage because they used it for tea. I thought that it tasted awful! But, of course, it is really good for you. Israel grew turkeys on giant turkey farms. but I never saw Arabs raise them. We had a big dinner at the Sunday school because we had a large kitchen and dining room up the road from the church. There was a little road between the Sunday school and the church. The Sunday school was housed on rental property. At the school we had a small refrigerator and a hotplate, so the teachers could put their own food in it.

My favorite Arab dish was grape leaves with rice called *warrock du wali* (pictured at left).

They also fixed something called *maqlooba*[19] or *maqluba* (pictured below). It was made of layered eggplant, meat, onions and rice, that had been cooked very slowly. After it was cooked they turned the pan upside down releasing the cooked mass, making it stand up like a cake. They also made something called *munsif* which was soaked bread in juice of lamb.

The village people ate a lot of goat, too, but it was more expensive than beef so was not eaten as often as other meats like chicken, which would normally be roasted whole over charcoal (*shashlik*). That was really delicious. Tiny doves, which were raised in cages like pets, provided a very tasty alternative. All of these meats were accompanied by a variety of boiled vegetables.

Our landlord's capable wife Um Majid had a stone with a wooden handle which was turned to grind wheat for special pastries. There were probably others who did this, but by this time, most women already used store-bought, self-rising flour for their pound cakes. They did use whole wheat for some of the breads. I think, by this time, most bought the flour even for their bread and didn't grind it themselves.

---

[19] These are transliterations from the Arabic script to our English letters so are approximations only.

The Arabs would eat *feta* cheese with their breads. Preserves were eaten with other foods but not with their bread. They made preserves (jam, not jelly) out of oranges, figs, dates and grapes. They didn't have *sur-jell* to make sure their preserves set, so Margaret would bring our teachers several boxes of *sur-jell* whenever she came home from the States.

Some of the people with more means used pots and pans from France and little enameled tea kettles. Other pots would be stainless steel or aluminum. When there were lots of people to cook for, they would use big aluminum kettles and cook outside, but most cooking was done on propane gas stoves inside.

Visiting Time

We lived in the Christian sector. So, of course, our landlord was a Christian and we were surrounded by Christian neighbors. The Arabs in Aboud were very hospitable, especially during holidays. They treated us like family. We could go to their houses without an invitation and they would do the same with us. Of course, we often visited church members and families of our students. We would knock politely before entering. Village people did not take off their shoes before going into the house; however, they did remove shoes to walk on carpets. Sometimes there were carpets, but more often, mats were laid on the beautiful stone tile floors.

Often, however, the villagers would be sitting on their veranda and we would just join them there. Their welcome in Arabic, *Ahalan wa Sahalan,* really meant 'take your ease'. If the neighbors were outside in the courtyard they would stand up when we came and offer us a seat. We would talk for a while and then they would bring us coffee or cola to drink with chocolate or English biscuits. They usually napped in the afternoon when it was hot, so we learned not to visit at those times. During summer, the children were not in school, so they also had to be quiet while their parents rested.

Sometimes our neighbors would tell us, 'Do you know how many pots of coffee we used this holiday?' They weren't complaining. They were bragging. It meant they had received many visitors. We quickly learned that when someone visits, you must always serve them something. We really enjoyed the special chocolate that they offered to guests.

One man in particular, Abu Majid, had a house that was built on a different level of the village. Their single daughter Majida cooked many meals for us. This family would sit on mats on the floor with little tables about 8 or 9 inches tall. Though we sat on those woven straw mats at their house, most homes had normal chairs or little 4-legged stools about a foot tall with woven bottoms to sit on.

If there was a baptismal service in the Greek Orthodox or Catholic churches, we would always be invited to come to their homes. We were considered important people in their village, so we would be invited for these special occasions. We were welcome to come any other time, as well. Lots of times they invited us for a meal. We were just one big family. They would also come to our house just to visit, and when they came, they would often bring someone with them. The youths came on Sunday afternoons to visit after the youth service, just to sit and talk.

Our Arab neighbors would shake hands when we entered their homes. If we met someone on the road, they would always shake our hands. We never looked at an older Muslim man in the eye. We were expected to look down. I would always greet them, but they would just nod their heads. Younger ones would shake my hand.

Food was special for holidays. We celebrated two Easters: the Orthodox one, the date of which changed every year, and the western one, as well as two Christmases: one in December and one in January. For Easter they prepared special cakes filled with dates. These were individual cakes with powdered sugar on the outside. One kind was called a 'crown of thorns' because it was circular and looked like a crown. It had slits, so you could see the figs or dates inside. Like the Israelis, the Arabs enjoyed a dessert called *halva*, which is very sweet, made of lots of almonds and honey. The Arabs, however, usually prefer cake, much like our pound cake.

As mentioned earlier, the meat was sometimes chicken, but usually goat or lamb roast. We thought goat tasted better, because it was not as greasy.

Of course, they like strong coffee served in tiny porcelain cups, sometimes with a metal holder, but often just a cup. If someone died, we had to drink this strong coffee without sugar. I thought that thick, strong coffee was awful, but I knew it was an honor to be served it. They also drank tea, made from loose tea, black, with sugar. During ordinary times they usually just served us Nescafe.

Shopping

If someone was going to kill an animal, they would bring it, kill it, gut it, and hang it on a tree between our house and the shop across the street so that people could come to buy different cuts. Because we had learned a lot about the parts of meat in school in America, we would say to the butcher, 'We want a kilo from here (pointing to the specific part) and then grind it into hamburger'. They would say, 'You don't use that kind of meat for ground meat!' They thought it was the choice part and shouldn't be used as ground meat – but they indulged us. Usually, however, we bought our meat at the supermarket in Jerusalem, which was about an hour's drive away and had meat already pre-cut and packaged.

The Christians worshipped on Sunday. The Muslims, of course, worshipped on Friday, but they didn't consider it a day when stores should be closed. Everything was open on Fridays and Sundays except offices which were closed on Fridays. Since offices were closed that day, they tried to get business done before Friday came. As Thursday ended, people could be seen scurrying around, preparing for their day of worship. If people had to go to the Israeli side, they knew shops were also closed on Saturday. Christian shop owners would close on Sunday mornings when they went to church.

The shop in front of our house was a family shop. In our village the young people would usually go to Ramallah, the county seat, to work. They were eager to get out of the village to make money. The owners of our shop didn't live at this location either. They lived at the other side of our village, which actually had only two shops. One was a Muslim shop, but I never went there. There may have been more, but I don't think so. You see, the Christians lived on one side and the Muslims lived on the other side. They weren't integrated, each living in their own sections, but they still interacted like a big family. The shop in front of us had a big room for flour, etc. They also had rice, canned goods, sugar, soft drinks, and beans. Everything was already packaged, except rice, which they would weigh out by the kilo. They sold mostly powdered milk, but fresh milk also came in plastic bags from warehouses in Ramallah. People didn't hang around inside the shop, but sometimes the older men could be seen sitting outside on the veranda, often playing backgammon. Mothers frequently sent their children to the store to get small items. We sometimes bought things there, but we did our major shopping at a supermarket in Jerusalem.

Agriculture

People had most fresh things growing in their own gardens. They didn't grow fruit like apples because it was too hot, but most of them had their own grape arbors, figs, olives, and date trees. There were two olive presses in the village that everyone could use. Dates were either dried or eaten straight off the tree.

A typical Arab family would have several hectares[20] of land, sometimes as many as 25. They all lived together in the village. Both men and women went out to the fields from the village to tend their crops. They told us that Israel had confiscated some of their land at the edge of the village, so they couldn't build houses near their crops. They mourned the loss of their land.

Everyone had olive, lemon, and almond trees. That's how they lived. The men were usually in the fields, plowing around the olive trees and watering the other trees. They didn't have enough water to water the olive trees – which are pretty tough anyway. Olive trees can withstand the dry, hot climate. They might number as many as 4000. Most people had a garden where the women grew eggplant, tomatoes, beans, small green squash like zucchini, potatoes, parsley, and cabbage. They didn't can any food, but they did bottle the olives. They had olive presses in the city, and they would sell the oil to Jordan, Ramallah, or Jaffa. Children would climb the olive trees and shake the olives onto burlap bags. Olives were harvested in October and sometimes as late as just before Christmas. These were sent to Jordan where they were pressed into oil and sold in the marketplaces.

Arab Generosity

Not only were Arabs hospitable, they were also generous. There was one poor woman who had several children. When the trucks came through selling produce, she would buy some and come with her children to our house. We would discover she had bought many kilos of potatoes or some other vegetable and often she had bought some for

---

[20] One hectare equals 2.471 acres

us, too. It was hard for us to accept those things, because we knew they didn't have much, but the smiles on their faces showed that giving gave them such joy. Whenever they baked bread, they would bring us bread, especially *pita* bread.

Our landlord was very generous also. Now Arabs don't give up their land: it must stay in the family. Our landlord, however, was exceptional. He gave land for the church to be built on. One time they mocked him for giving the property for the church. 'Don't tell us she (Margaret) didn't pay for that property.' He replied, 'Oh yes, I was paid in ways that you wouldn't understand. I've received more blessings than you would ever understand, too.'

Aboud had both a Muslim and a Christian mayor which was unusual. Most villages would be one or the other. In addition to this division, they were divided into tribes or families. In the case of Aboud, I'm not sure how many Muslim tribes there were, but I knew there were at least two Christian tribes: *Fuadli* and *Bisharia*. Disputes were decided by the head of the tribe in consultation with the elders – that is, each mayor with the senior adult males decided issues for their own people. One time when we wanted to buy extra property, the elders discussed it among themselves and told us the result. We didn't see any public meetings to decide issues. We were careful not to get into arguments with people and would stay out of arguments among the men, in particular.

Arab Family Life

The Arabic family is strongly patriarchal. Women's expectations when they married were to be good wives and mothers and to fulfill the expectations of their husbands without debate. They were expected to work hard and produce children. To be fair, however, not all Muslim men were hard on their women. Many treated their wives wonderfully. Who was responsible for the home? Several women worked outside the home, and since so many of the husbands were in America, most women had to do everything. However, the man was definitely the head of the house. I observed that as long as the woman was producing children and providing meals, men didn't interfere with household matters. We were requested to visit a Muslim man once, the mayor of the Muslim section of the village, and the wife didn't even make an appearance. We were served by the daughters, but after they served us even they also went out.

Christian women dressed similar to the picture at the right. The full-length belted dresses were usually beige – or black and white, with red hand-embroidery. One could identify the Ramallah district by the belt. Their embroidered white-on-white nylon headdresses were made from woven silk-like fabric made in Switzerland.

The dresses pictured above cost about $200 each. After they no longer looked good enough for dress-up, these beautiful dresses were sometimes worn for everyday work around the house. The headdresses were worn only for special occasions because they were very elaborate and expensive.

Everyone was like family. You could say whatever you wanted. Because everyone was so friendly, they included us; and I never once felt homesick. I found that as long as I was doing God's will, I never suffered from homesickness.

Why Aboud?

People wonder why Margaret picked out Aboud for our ministry. The village certainly was nothing special. It happened this way: Margaret was in Jerusalem at the church on the Mount of Olives when a man who was helping out in the church told her, 'I'm going to take you to a true Arab village'. In that village, Aboud, she met a blind lady named Zariefe.

Zariefe knew English because she had attended an English-speaking school for the blind in Bethlehem as a child. For years she had been praying for a Protestant missionary to come to Aboud. Margaret had been traveling back and forth from Amman to Bethlehem and Jerusalem, but Zariefe had been praying that Margaret would come to Aboud. So it came about that the Lord confirmed to Margaret that Aboud was where she should be. Zariefe became very important to us as an interpreter.

Arlene and Zariefe visiting in an Arab home.

5

ABOUD PRIMARY SCHOOL

When I arrived in Aboud in 1973, I began teaching school immediately and later taught, also, in the Sunday school. We had to follow the curriculum that the Jordanians set up for their schools – they told us how many hours of social studies, etc., we needed. I taught English to grades 4, 5 and 6 in the Aboud Primary School, which consisted of 15 classrooms and was located up the road from the church. I was

Arlene and Margaret at the dedication of the new school building in September, 1973 with the one male Arab teacher (right of Margaret), children and parents who attended the dedication.

teaching the children English and the teachers also wanted to practice English, so I was hindered from learning the Arabic language. I did take some Arabic lessons in Bethlehem so that I knew the Arabic letters and could understand if my interpreter was not interpreting properly, but I always felt disappointed with myself that I wasn't fluent in Arabic.

We did a lot of acting out of the lessons. I admit to being a bit of an actress! The students had composition, dictation and writing. No napping at our school! Even the kindergarten children would go to school until 3 or 4 in the afternoon without a nap.

Miss Rima Azar, Arabic; Miss Laila Hamid, Math; Iftihar Masad, kindergarten; Sister Arlene, Suhaila Khoury; Miss Aida Masad, Science; Miss Somaya, English. Trip to Greece as a reward to the teachers.

When the children arrived in the morning, if it was not raining (and it did not rain often), the children would play outside until a bell rang. Then all the children lined up with their teacher and went up the stairs to their home rooms where attendance was taken. Afterwards they went to the chapel for 'opening exercises'. The chapel was about as big as the church. Opening chapel was led by Margaret, Miss Raika,[21] or another of the Arab teachers and now, of course, Suhaila.[22]

The children sat on wooden benches which had backs. (I learned how to repair benches, mix cement, lay stone tile – we had to do all of that.) The children did a lot of singing in chapel, but we didn't have music classes. Their favorite songs were, 'Go Tell It on the Mountain', and 'My Heart Is Happy Because I'm Walking with the King'. We presented stories with flashcard pictures like, 'The Little Red Hen', telling how the little red hen gave her life by sheltering the little chicks under her feathers. Sometimes they would have contests to see who could say the most scripture verses. Always, we closed with the Lord's Prayer.

All classes were departmentalized. The teachers would rotate, not the children. There were lower and upper kindergartens for 4- and 5-year-old students downstairs. They had their opening chapel in each of their own rooms. The upper grades, from one to six, went up the stairs to their classrooms. There were usually about six to eight teachers. It was strange to me that even first graders had different teachers for every subject, but this was necessary because not everyone could teach everything, especially English. They had one teacher for math, one for English, one for social studies, and one for Arabic. The only Muslim man teacher taught some of the Arabic classes because he really knew the grammar well. We probably had 80 students or so in the upper grades with 10 or 11 in each class. In kindergarten, the classes were bigger because we had children from other surrounding villages. We probably had 80 or so students in the upper grades with 10 or 11 in each class.

There was also a Catholic and a government school in our village of 3,000 people. Both Christian and Muslim children attended our school through sixth grade. Most of the Muslim children not only attended our regular school but also Sunday school as well.

---

[21] Raika Ibrahim Khalil Khoury
[22] Suhaila El Koury is the principal of the school now.

We had a special Sunday school on the lower floor of Abu Saleh's house on Wednesdays for the Muslim children because they couldn't come to the church. This was voluntary, of course, but the children liked it.

After finishing sixth grade, Christian kids who could afford to go to a private school went to the Friends school in Ramallah, or the Mennonite school in Bethlehem. If they couldn't afford that, they went to the government school in the village. Most students who left us and went to the government schools would stop us on the road and tell us how much they remembered and appreciated what we had taught them. They would say, 'We cannot do anything about it now because we are living at home, but we remember what you taught us'. When some got ready to emigrate to the United States, they would ask us for a Bible to take with them.

It was, of course, illegal for us to proselytize but we did anyway, and the Jordanian government ignored us because of the high-quality education we provided. It was not allowed to teach a Muslim student the Christian religion, but I was always thrilled to hear the Muslim children singing, 'I'm Walking with the King' and other Christian songs. Some of the parents knew English – especially the principal of the government school – so they understood what the children were learning. We were so happy that we were given a permanent school license because the government didn't normally do that. We didn't even apply. They thought the quality of our education was so high, they just gave it to us.

We, of course, had government inspectors who came to all the classes every year and listened to us. From what they saw, they gave us this permanent school license, but they came every year to inspect us anyway. The teachers were required to hand the lesson plan book over to the inspectors when they came in. Sometimes teachers would try to give a lesson they had taught the day before, but that was not acceptable. That's why they had to hand their books over. One of my happiest moments was when we got that permanent license. It was permanent until we got a new superintendent from Amman, Jordan. After that we had to apply every year.

Though the school term followed the Jordanian rules, classes began in September, as in the United States, and ended in May, which left a long summer break. We had a color-coded schedule for the whole school posted downstairs. Each teacher had a color, which made for a very colorful bulletin board.

Tasty Enough to Be Eaten

We didn't serve meals to the children. They brought their own food from home. Everyone ate his/her packed lunch outside. Of course, there was always a teacher on duty. There were 15 rooms, so there were a lot of children outside, but I don't remember any violence among them. It seldom rained, so that was not a problem. The children would often bring pita bread to school with olive oil and *zaatar* (thyme) on it. There were children who wanted to spend time with me, especially on the playground. They would want to cling to me, so I would tell them, 'You're going to go on until I can eat my clothes with all this oil on them'.

I was an experienced teacher, having already taught for eight years in the United States. If you ask me how these kids were different from American kids, I would say, 'Kids are kids'. I loved teaching, especially the fourth grade. I had brought flip charts from the U.S. – about 20 x 24 inches – which had the letters, vowels, sounds, etc., in English. We also had illustrations from the Thompson Chain Bible, maps and footprints of Jesus, etc. We had flash cards for English and math, and we had an old-fashioned hand spirit duplicator[23] that we used to copy hand-drawn materials. One man at Mt. Paran Church in Atlanta, who works in the top level of education said, 'I don't know how you are doing it all. You are training the teachers as well as the students. Just writing curriculum and preparing materials is a full-time job.' We were so happy when we got a long-carriage word processor because we were writing everything by hand – sometimes 100 letters a month as well as the lessons.

Margaret made one chart about which I asked, 'How did you learn to do that?' She laughed and said, 'I made it before that company did in the USA'. The English books came from England; and, of course, they utilizeds British spellings. The Arabic books were probably printed in Ramallah, but may have been ordered from Amman, Jordan. They were all paperbacks.

---

[23] Readers who have been born during the computer era may not have ever seen one of these which had a liquid gelatin bed which was used to produce a blue copy of whatever was put on it. It was a tedious and time-consuming process.

The children had to buy their own books and had lots of homework, so they would put their notebooks and paperbacks into their backpacks and take them home. They had exercises to do in composition, dictation, writing, etc. One can still see Arab kids everywhere reciting their lessons, parading on the flat roofs of their homes. The Arab way of teaching was strictly memorization, but we tried to use teaching methods other than just memorizing.

We didn't teach any practical classes, because they learned those things at home. All of the girls knew how to sew, knit, embroider, crochet, cook, etc. The boys learned carpentry, etc., from their fathers. One unusual thing about our school was that the school was mixed – boys and girls together. Our teachers were all women, except for the one man, because they were the ones available to us. By contrast, the teachers who taught in the government school were all men except for one woman, but they even sent their own children to our school because of the quality of education. The children paid minimal tuition – about $10 a year.

Bible Lessons

All of the children studied the Bible even though they were almost all Muslims. As I said, the supervising authorities in Amman just ignored this because our level of education was so superior to that of other schools.

In Grade 1, they studied the *Journeys of Jesus*, some of his parables, the footprints of his last days, along with Psalm 23 and Psalm 150. Grade 2 studied Jesus' life, his journeys, some of his miracles, the footprints of his last days, along with Psalm 1 and Psalm 8. Grade 3 studied *Acts: The Journeys of Paul*, along with Psalm 19, Psalm 24 and Psalm 27. Grade 4 studied Genesis, Exodus, Leviticus, Numbers and Deuteronomy, along with Psalm 51, Psalm 32, and Psalm 34. Grade 5 studied the books of Joshua through 2 Chronicles, along with Psalm 42, Psalm 46, and Psalm 126. Grade 6 studied Revelation, the 'Big Prophets', the 'Small Prophets', the Apostles and prophecies, along with Psalm 91, Psalm 100, and Psalm 103. I should mention that they had to memorize each of these Psalms. The Acts of the Apostles class is where we used the maps in the Thompson's Chain Reference Bibles showing all the footprints where the apostles went.

Evaluations

We had regular report cards and evaluated students every six weeks, just like in America, but we had to meet all the standards of the Jordanian government. When our students went to other schools for secondary school, they had to prepare for the senior exam that all Jordanian students have to take. Students who studied with us at the lower levels consistently did well on that senior exam.

Recess

When the children went outside at recess, they played soccer on a cement court. Many times, I'd be outside painting lines for their soccer field. I couldn't tolerate too much sun, so Margaret would have to check on me every now and then to make sure I'd not passed out because it was so hot. One day I got hit in the head with a soccer ball. Mercy, that ball was hard! I even had to teach soccer, and I didn't know anything about soccer. Thank God, we had an encyclopedia because I didn't have the slightest idea how to teach that sport. The girls played soccer, too.

We taught them basketball and tether ball. When I'd see them fall down on that cement and skin their knees, I'd need to get out the iodine from the first aid kit. Nothing really serious ever happened, however. Isn't that amazing?

Programs

We had very good school celebrations at the church. We chose one guy to be 'Jesus' for the Easter program. The teacher didn't seem to understand why we had chosen him, because of his long hair, because she had his hair cut the day of the program!

Normally, the teachers helped a lot, especially Raika. She was the oldest of the teachers and taught a lot of the religion classes. All of the teachers didn't attend our church but she and her niece Suhaila did. The programs were basically Bible stories. In one Easter pageant, 'Jesus' had to be put in the tomb. They couldn't get 'Jesus' into the altar (where hymn books were normally kept), so they just sort of 'stuffed' the crucified 'Jesus' into the space under the altar – the 'tomb'. Yes, they just folded him up and 'stuffed' him in! They didn't know what else to do. It was hilarious.

The parents would come to watch. Sometimes funny things happened. At one Easter program, a soldier was standing at the tomb. An elderly family member got out her handkerchief and went up front to wipe the nose of that soldier in the middle of the pageant!

We had pageants for Christmas and Easter and a parade on Palm Sunday which was my favorite time because they all lined up outside with braided palm leaves and bouquets of flowers. They would march around the church three times, once each, for the 'Father, Son and Holy Spirit'. You see, most of the Christians were Greek Orthodox or Roman Catholic and they were used to a lot of pomp and ceremony. The children stopped on the last round and laid their flowers on the altar and sang songs.

Arlene's favorite pageant: Psalm Sunday procession

We had one Italian Catholic priest who actually urged the children to come to our Sunday school. He said, 'They really learn the Bible there'. We didn't force any of the students to come to the church – they just wanted to, especially for the pageants. Most of the pageants of the school were held at the church, even the school programs.

Becoming Principal

When Margaret asked me to be the principal, I begged her, saying, 'Not yet. I don't know Arabic well enough', but she said, 'You would always say that. I want to spend more time at the church.' She even had a gavel made for me for the meetings and said, 'Now you are doing it'. So, I became the principal. I had Suhaila, one of the kindergarten teachers who had received the baptism of the Holy Spirit and had attended Bethlehem College (at my urging), to help me. Without her help I could not have made it.

Talking to the parents was difficult, but I would bring Suhaila in with me. We had one high-strung mother whose boys were trouble makers. They would complain about the one Muslim teacher at the school. I counseled Suhaila, 'Don't get angry with her, just reach out and hold her hand'. I don't think I ever got through to Suhaila about the purpose of that gesture. And no matter what happened, the mother would always become very dramatic.

The most difficult part of the job was my own language limitations. I had to rely on Suhaila to help me in that as well. Margaret studied for the English-Arabic test for which she needed to go to London, but she never got the opportunity to do it. Nor did I ever endeavor to do that. I would use some games with the children, though, like writing in English and then I would transliterate a whole paragraph and they would have to read it with English letters but with Arabic sounds. I would say, '*Inzel ila'l idara w' coola* sister *aateni mlabas men fudlic!*' (Go to the office and tell sister you want a sweet!) They had fun with this language game.

Excelling as a School

As I mentioned previously, the school's curriculum had to measure up to Jordanian standards. We had to get our permit to operate renewed every year, but since our school was so good, the government gave us a permanent license. It was considered the best school in all of Jordan.

We had one girl who could write exactly as I did. Her penmanship was excellent. You see, one of the things we ordinarily taught was writing, and they had to learn to write well. This girl had great potential. She's now married to a pastor in Bethlehem.

We made a social studies textbook for our students in grade 4. Even the Jordanians didn't have one. They were impressed. We used American lesson plans with objectives, etc., including behavioral objectives. Our teachers were required not only to submit the lesson plans, they had to prove that they had accomplished the plan. As I said earlier, we had to fit into the Jordanian system in every other way.

We had a little library, and the children loved to check out the English library books because the Arabic ones were so difficult. They would come after school to choose books or the teacher would take them down to the library as a group.

Aboud Primary School, which was built in 1973.

A New Minister of Education

When a new minister of education was appointed in Amman, we feared that we would have to release all the Muslim children from the school. The administrator in Ramallah called and said, 'I have ignored that you are proselytizing Muslim children, but with the new minister of education in this position, you could lose your license'. The administration really wanted us to teach Muslim history and religion in our school. They didn't want us to lose our students because many of their own children attended our school. In fact, the Muslim principal called me to the Muslim school to speak to the male teachers who left their classes to talk to me. They said, 'We appreciate you more than the Christians do'. They begged me not to release the children out of our school. The supervisor even offered to pay for the principal or teacher if we would teach Muslim history and religion. I said, 'How can we allow money to be paid for something we don't believe in. God would take his blessing away from us. Even our own church doesn't support any primary schools. If you let me come and teach Sunday school classes at the mosque, then I will let you come and teach at our school.' They looked amused and then started laughing because they knew that was not going to happen.

They said, 'You are smart'.

I replied, 'I knew you wouldn't let me'.

All the other schools except one Catholic school allowed the Muslim religion to be taught, but we did not. This shocked the whole country. Even the Christian schools were shocked by our response because they allowed Islam to be taught. They said, 'They'll kill that woman (me)'. We eventually had to release half of our students – those that were Muslim.

Until today, however, Muslim children are coming from the surrounding villages to attend kindergarten at our school because they don't have kindergartens. We still cannot accept Muslim students for the higher grades.

Visitors

Many people would come to visit the school. One special couple was E.L. and Doris Turner, long-time pastor friends from Kannapolis, North Carolina. When they visited, they would ask, 'Do your teachers like junk food?'[24]

I replied, 'Why don't you ask them'. After that, whenever they visited, they brought chips and other snacks for the teachers that the teachers loved and eagerly looked forward to.

Turning Things Over

After I had worked ten years just as a teacher and then ten years as both a teacher and principal, the overseer made the final decision to turn the school over to an Arab. We had an Arab pastor and I had been training an Arab woman, Suhaila, to head the school. Margaret would have preferred another woman, but Suhaila was trained at

---

[24] Snacks, chips, etc.

Bethlehem College and the other woman had no college training. Suhaila was very able. I would present a problem to her: 'What would you do here? That's good that you know that, but you need to tell me, *why* you would do that?' She could always tell me why. Margaret listened to me and we agreed that Suhaila would be the one. She was good. So good, in fact, that she's been principal there now about 40 years.

Dinner at Margaret and Arlene's home: Back row, left: Gabi Schmidgall, (hidden Sebastian Schmidgall), Raika, and Suhaila. Front row, left: Margaret, Butros Mualem, Isam Bejali, and Amadeus Schmidgall.

6

ABOUD CHURCH AND SUNDAY SCHOOL

Margaret did everything in the church except teach Sunday school. While she was preaching to the adults, someone else was teaching the children. Zariefe, the little blind lady, interpreted for Margaret until Margaret became fluent in Arabic. Later, when I preached, Suhaila interpreted for me. When the overseer came he would preach in German. Translating from his German into Arabic was a very difficult task for Margaret, but she managed.

Aboud Church

Teaching Sunday School

I taught lessons in the Sunday school using David Cook's comic book-type Arab books. This made it easy because I could ask questions based on what they were reading.

Every time I'd go to get my visa renewed, the Jordanian authority would ask me what I was doing in Aboud. I'd say, 'You know very well what I'm doing in that village'.

The Muslims would ask, 'What are you here for? You are pro-Israeli.' Those were very difficult and dangerous times.

God's Hand At Work

Not everything, however, was negative. There were times in which God made himself known in unexpected ways. There was a young man who lived across the street from the church. This man was living a normal life when he suddenly became very sick. His head became enlarged, and he would just sit and stare. The doctors in Ramallah could do nothing for him. So, they sent him to the big Jewish hospital in Jerusalem. Since the family didn't speak English, the doctors there told me to tell the mother, who insisted her son would get well, 'Sister, you've got to get them to realize this man is going to die'. Now I knew his mother would never accept that possibility.

The only time we would see any reaction from the young man was when we sang Arabic hymns to him. His eyes would start moving, looking for the source of the music. The hospital finally sent him home to die, but the mother kept insisting that he was not going to die. One day I stopped on my way home from school. I knelt down beside his cot and prayed for him. I could see by the look on his face that songs like, 'I Live for Jesus Day to Day' ministered to him. This went on for a couple of weeks. Shortly thereafter, I went home on leave and Margaret had returned from her leave.

Every church in Aboud had a bell – the Roman Catholics, the Orthodox church, and our church. One Sunday morning as the church bells were ringing, the young man opened his eyes and said, out of the clear blue, 'I want to go to church'. As you can imagine, the family was shocked, but two people walked with him on either side as they started to cross over the street to our church.

Margaret told me that the people were already assembled when he came walking into the church. Margaret told me, 'You should have seen the reaction of the people!' He was completely and absolutely healed. After that, he married and had children. He also opened a store; and when Margaret went home on furlough, she brought back some equipment to help him to start a photography shop.

There was a baby who had a growth on its leg that was also instantly healed. God was not absent!

Linda Hickey came to help me for one year when Margaret finally got a proper home leave. Linda and I would go to Jerusalem once a week. Usually, we'd have a routine: first we'd have lunch at a restaurant that we liked, then we'd go to the supermarket, and just before we went home, we'd get our mail. One time, Linda said, 'Let's get our mail first before we eat so we can be reading our mail while we eat'. If we'd not gotten our mail first that day, we would have been in an explosion in that very good Arab restaurant where we had planned to eat. Some Israelis would eat there, and the bomb was the Arab way of saying, 'We don't want you here'. There were other times we went to Jerusalem and we'd find out later that there was a demonstration in 'such and such' a place on our route, and we knew we would automatically have been caught in the crossfire. There were many things that God did through those years to assure us of his presence with us.

It was very rare for people to receive the Baptism of the Holy Spirit. Worship was very sedate, perhaps because they came from an Orthodox background. We planted many seeds, especially among our students.

Parents would often come for prayer. There were two other churches in Aboud and they often attended their services, but when they had a need for prayer, they would come to us. They would bring their children up front at the church services for prayer even though they were members of other churches. Greek Orthodox priests' children were in our schools, as well.

There were many shared concerns for the community. People in this community helped one another by pouring cement for the roof of a house that was being built. Rather than give money, they gave of themselves. They, also, would help older people in the community harvest olives. This was a good example to us.

Does God Love The Sinner?

One concept that was very difficult for all of the children to understand was the love of God. Margaret once taught a whole series on how God loves the sinner. She got to the end of the story. 'Does God love the sinner?' Margaret asked. 'No, sister. He doesn't love the sinner', they would answer.

To the Arab mind it was just inconceivable that God could love sinners. For the Muslim, they were always trying to balance their good deeds with their bad deeds – praying the good ones would outnumber the bad ones. Even the Christian Arabs were convinced that God does not love the sinner until they were born-again or baptized.

Home Leave Time

Previously, I've told you about times when the LORD gave me discernment about certain people and situations. One time, while serving in Aboud, I was back in the USA on furlough. I was driving down I-75 going to Cleveland, Tennessee, when I saw a vision of a Church of God official who had experienced much heartache and grief. He had suffered a stroke. In my vision I saw a brief view of him in his house. He was struggling to button his shirt. Now I really needed to check out what I had seen. I wanted to be sure that he was having such a difficult time before I said anything. I was sure enough about what I had seen in this vision, however, that I bought a frame, some black velvet, and a card of shirt buttons. I glued the shirt buttons to the black velvet and put it in the frame which had a little tripod to make it stand.

When I arrived in Cleveland, I went to this man's office, hoping to encourage him by telling him about my vision. As we started talking, I asked him how he was doing. 'I want to know something,' I said. (I was always hesitant, afraid I might be wrong). 'What is the hardest thing for you to do since you had your stroke?' He promptly said, 'Buttoning my shirt'.

Meanwhile, I was reaching for the gift bag on the floor. He laughed and said, 'You keep handling that bag. What is in there?'

'Were they little buttons like these?' I asked, as I brought out the framed buttons on the velvet. He just looked at me.

Then I said, 'In a vision I saw you trying to button your shirt. If God can see the little things we need, then he can see the other big things in your life.'

He said, 'I'm going keep that on that little tripod here in my office to remind me that God sees me.'

Another time, when I was home on furlough, I preached at my cousin Eleanor's Methodist church in Sinking Springs, Ohio. After I finished preaching, Eleanor and her husband pointed out that there was one particular girl in the congregation to whom I had really ministered.

'You just ploughed her row', Eleanor said. In other words, I had really hit that girl hard, and things she was praying about were answered in the sermon. I often experienced that people received answers from God when I preached.

Home Away from Home

I still consider Israel home. They've asked me to send my heart back there when I die. I'm not going to, but I still stay in contact with several people to this day.

At that time, though there were only two telephones in the village, those belonging to the priest and the mayor, Suhaila called me frequently. She still does. Another one calls me from Aboud and some others, who went to Wisconsin to study, still call me.

7

TRANSITION

Now a missionary should, if possible, work herself out of a job. After I had been principal for ten years, the overseer, Paul Schmidgall, who was getting ready to leave Israel to become president of the European Bible Seminary in Germany, decided that he wanted an Arab pastor to head the church as well as an Arab teacher to head the school.[25] Since his goal was for everything to be run by Arabs in Aboud, he wanted both the church and the school to be put into Arab hands by the time he left. I understood that, but what I didn't understand was the process used to terminate my work. When I prepared for home leave the last time, we had already put Suhaila in charge of the school while I was away. Usually my home leave was for a year, but this time I only planned to be away six months.

Towards the end of that six-month furlough, my dad received a letter for me from World Missions, telling me that my work in Aboud had come to an end. He cried because he knew how I would feel. We were both devastated. I really expected I'd be in Aboud forever. I had taken all of my personal things there – my pictures and treasured things. It was painful. I understood that Suhaila would now be the principal, but I expected that I would stay on to finish some curriculum work for three or four months, at least, and then serve alongside as needed. I felt there were tasks that were not completed. There were

---

[25] We had often sent people to Germany or to the United States to train at the Bible school, but they didn't want to return. Of course, there was always trouble between Jews and Arabs and there was terrorism; so, they saw going to Germany or America as a way out of a difficult situation.

still Sunday school curricula to write and some additional things in English needed to be completed for the school.

Your Mission is Finished

The church in Aboud now had an Arab pastor and an Arab principal. I knew, however, that the Arabs would not accept Suhaila unless I was the one to turn the school over to her officially. They would all wonder what had happened and wouldn't respect Suhaila in that position unless I prepared to go back and personally turn the work over to her. I remained in the States for the rest of my furlough and then flew back to Aboud.

I arrived before school started in September of 1993. I resumed my duties as Suhaila and I had planned and prepared to leave before Christmas, just in time for the new semester. It was a very hard time for me. When the teachers found out about my leaving, they were upset, too; but for reasons I didn't understand, God was moving me on.

Farewell

Before I left, Margaret arranged a special service at the church. The superintendent, Paul Schmidgall, came and spoke and others talked about the good things I had done. Bishara Awad, headmaster of the renowned Mennonite school in Bethlehem gave a tribute. Bishara had helped a lot of our missionaries as an interpreter. I felt honored that he would speak.

When someone leaves they always say nice things like people do at a funeral. And it felt like a funeral for me. Of course, they sang and had special prayers for me on that particular day.

There was a reception at the school where they served coffee and coke and Arab pastries and there was a big beautiful flower arrangement from Margaret. People gave me presents. Paul and Gabi Schmidgall gave me one of those beautiful, low, brass and teakwood coffee tables. People from Bethlehem and Nazareth came. A lot of them were crying. One man, who had just gotten home from Amman where he had bought a new head piece for himself, gave it to me instead. As he put it around my shoulders, he apologized that he hadn't known I was leaving, so he didn't have time to prepare anything for me. It was very touching.

The teachers had gone together and gotten me six copies of desert scenes in watercolor by David Roberts. They were very sad I was leaving, but the time had come for me to go.

Paul Schmidgal, overseer, and son, with Abu Majid, the giver of the land for the church (the goat was named Arlene, not exactly an honor!)

Packing Up

Fortunately, I waited to pack my things until after the farewell. I needed to find a way to send my things back, including my lovely gifts. We realized I couldn't send things through the Tel Aviv airport from Aboud because nothing from the Arab territories was allowed to pass there, so I went to a friend's house in Jerusalem on the Israeli side where two American missionaries helped me to pack all of my things which were then to be sent by air to Ohio. These missionaries kindly let me use their return address so that there would be no problems with the Israeli authorities.

Finding a New Field

World Missions thought they would send me somewhere else to teach, but they didn't realize that I didn't have the Bible and theology qualifications to teach in a seminary or Bible school. The board asked me where I wanted to go next. I suggested, 'Look, there are two or three places where I would consider teaching, but', I added, 'one thing I can tell you: South America – no. I don't even have to pray about it.' I couldn't imagine going to such a 'laid-back' culture; I'm very German. I want it done 'yesterday'. Who would have thought that it was exactly where I would go? I was thinking about winning sinners to the Lord in a completely different culture and I would never have had the patience to do that – but to teach the 'cream of the crop', that was different!

World Missions didn't know where to put me. Mary Ruth Stone asked Philip Morris if I could teach a short course at the European Bible Seminary (EBS) for her on 'activities for church people'. He agreed, so I went there during my waiting time. I taught the intensive course, but it didn't work out very well. There were things I suggested in the course that I would do, only to find out they wouldn't work well in Germany. The girl whom they got to interpret for me was actually a student in the course and she didn't really know English. After about the third day one of the faculty said, 'Arlene, I know you. I can tell you what students are giving you trouble.' Though someone who had the needed credentials could have 'signed off' for me on my courses, I knew EBS was not a place I could stay and teach.

I also taught a course at Lee College on the introduction to Islam as a part of Ridley Usherwood's evangelism course. I couldn't continue teaching there, of course. They had strict standards, and I had only a master's degree. Furthermore, my master's degree was in the wrong subject area. I needed another place.

Home Again

I flew back to Cincinnati, Ohio, where I had a mobile home, but it was rented out. Since the transition was so sudden, we'd not had time to prepare the renter, so I had to stay with my mom and dad in their small, two-bedroom house.

My mother told someone, 'I feel so sorry for Arlene. She decides she's going to wear something and discovers it is stored somewhere else.'

You see, I had things stored at my sister's house in Lexington, Kentucky; and I also had things stored at my other sister's house in Cincinnati, because my parents didn't have room for my things and theirs, too.

A New Idea

After arriving back home in March of 1994, I started evangelizing and raising money for Aboud. At that time, I wasn't sure where I was going next. I always raised money not only for myself, but also – especially – for the school. Grant McClung got in touch with me.[26] He had an idea that was to change my life. Someone had told him that John Hayes[27] needed a person to train missionaries in South America to reach the Muslim world with the Gospel. Grant prayed about it first, then he approached me with the idea. 'You are the only person in our church that has even lived in the Arab world. You are the person who is best able to train those missionaries.' He was right. Our village was half Muslim and half Christian, so I had had lots of experience.

I was raising funds in Florida and North Carolina when World Missions told me that, indeed, I would be going to the World Evangelism Action Center (WEAC) to help John. My insurance had expired, and my missionary salary had paused, but I was still itinerating. Most states in the denomination didn't have health insurance for the missionaries at that time. Thank God, the Church of God Office in Ohio had a health insurance program, but I had not paid into it, so I was not eligible to receive help from them, either. God sent the Turners,[28] with whom I had been staying, to the rescue. They said, 'Our church is going to pay your health insurance until you find out where

---

[26] Grant McClung was the professor of missions at the School of Theology at that time.

[27] John Hayes was the director of the World Evangelism Action Center, later know as the Missionary Training Center in São Paulo, Brazil at that time.

[28] Elmer and Doris Turner pastored for many years in North Carolina. At that time they were pastoring the Valdese Church of God.

you are going next in ministry'. They paid my insurance costs/fees for about a year.

Studying Again

I needed to study to be able to teach in South America. I took New Testament Survey, Introduction to World Missions, and one other course at our Church of God Theological Seminary in Cleveland, Tennessee. Grant McClung suggested that the best place for me to study about Islam would be with Zwemer Institute for Muslim Studies in Pasadena, California.[29] This institute was not connected with only one denomination. They also had several experts. One was Dr Robert Douglas. Dr Douglas helped me so much: he was a practical man who gave us many notes and allowed his students to copy his materials. He encouraged me greatly.

I studied two courses on Islam at the Bethel Bible College, an Assembly of God school in Springfield, Missouri, under the auspices of Zwemer and taught by Dr Douglas. Each course consisted of one week of intensive studies: one on the Bible (Revelation and the Qur'an), and the other on Arab culture. The Zwemer Center gave me lots of credit because of my experience in Aboud. The professors didn't stay in Pasadena. They traveled, like we students did, to wherever the courses were being taught. For the completion of these courses I received a special certificate in Islamic Studies. These fine professors influenced me greatly. It was a very encouraging time.

Remember the sanctification that I believe in? Well, the director at the Assemblies of God school where I took these courses with Dr Douglas knew that in the Church of God we believe that a person is totally sanctified at a specific time, while the Assemblies of God believe it is a continuous work of grace. The director of their Bible school in Springfield walked in one day when Dr Douglas was teaching. When Ron walked in, he said, 'Listen here, you Assemblies of God people (he was one himself), you have to respect Arlene – she really has the baptism of the Holy Ghost, because Church of God people don't get it until they've been sanctified wholly'. They all laughed.

---

[29] It is now called Zwemer Center for Muslim Studies and is located in Columbia International University, South Carolina. www.zwemercenter.com.

Another professor was Dr Phil Parshall. I was so touched by his humble demeanor; yet, he was very intelligent, witty and quite a philosophical student of the Muslims. When Dr Parshall and his wife, Julie, invited me to their home for a meal, I saw that it was a very simple home. In fact, Dr Parshall's office was the center of his bed!

In connection with Zwemer, I took another course, a basic missionary training course at the Summer Institute of Linguistics (SIL) with Wycliffe Bible Translators headquarters in a Dallas, Texas, suburb. SIL put their own prospective missionaries through this basic training because their missionaries go to very primitive places. When the trainers explained what we had to do, I could immediately relate. I'd experienced all of those things. The other candidates asked me, 'Did you write the course?' Our professors were very knowledgeable about living in other cultures. Some professors had served in Africa and some in India.

I also completed a course in Ontario, Canada. In total I finished about 25 hours of studies in Muslim ministries. Although I had agreed to study only because I needed to have some qualifications for my work in South America, I thoroughly enjoyed all my studies.

8

ITINERATING IN GRIEF

As I itinerated, I finished writing a sixth grade English book for Aboud. I had to live, so when I would receive an offering at a church where I was speaking, I used that money to live on, and the pledges that were given at the church were always for Aboud.

But I was so much in grief. Leaving Aboud had been hard. My parents didn't even know how difficult it was for me. Ginny Mullinax and I were eating out one day at Baskin-Robbins in Cleveland. Ginny's pretty swift, also. She didn't know the story, but she said, 'Arlene, you are grieving so much God can't get through to you about what he wants you to do in South America'. I knew it was from the Lord. At least someone understood, and I needed to prepare for a new period of my life.

9

SOUTH AMERICA

I didn't realize it at the time, but God was preparing me for a wider ministry – for a whole continent. The Lord was showing me this bigger picture by taking me to South America. I've become more aware of it from a distance because I could see how my work in South America was not only preparing people for the foreign field but also for their own ministries to Muslims in their own countries. Many of them went on not only to foreign countries but to pastor churches, to be youth directors and active Christians who reached Muslims in their own areas. They also taught discipleship and spiritual warfare courses themselves.

John Hayes, the director of the World Evangelism Action Center (WEAC),[30] recalls that he was teaching a course at the School of Theology in Cleveland, Tennessee,[31] when Dr Grant McClung approached him about me. He didn't know me, but immediately he realized, as had Grant, that I could be of help to them in South America with my wide experience with Arabs. He was aware that there were many Arabs in South America and that they and many other kinds of Muslims needed to be reached with the Gospel.

---

[30] See appendix E for information about what WEAC, later the Missionary Training Center (MTC-CTM in Portuguese), sought to do in South America. In the document, the Missionary Training Center is referred to both in English as MTC and Portuguese as CTM (Centro de Treinamento Missionário).

[31] Later, Church of God Theological Seminary, and now Pentecostal Theological Seminary.

São Paulo, Brazil

After I celebrated Christmas with my family, it was time for me to go to South America. In January, 1994, I flew to São Paulo, Brazil, and was met at the airport by John. The first Sunday after my arrival in South America, I was attending a Portuguese-speaking congregation, but inside I was rebelling and telling God, 'I'm supposed to be singing in Arabic'.

Much to my surprise, however, I discovered that South America was full of Arabs and other Muslims – many, especially, from Lebanon. Of course, there are many differences between Arabs from various countries: differences in food, traditions, etc. For example, I discovered there are a lot of Arabs in Venezuela and in Chile where there are many Christian Arabs as well as Muslim. I discovered the wonderful fact that the people I loved were in South America, too.

John explained to me that WEAC opened in 1985 in São Paulo, Brazil, but people in South America did not understand that term. So, in 1990 it was re-named Missionary Training Center (CTM in Portuguese). The center was designed to train Latin American missionaries, but there were many Lee College[32] students attending at first. I was invited to visit in 1994 to see if I wanted to come and help them. I not only went to visit: I came and stayed until 2009, when I broke my neck!

Teaching in South America

I was at the Missionary Training Center (MTC) from January through March where I taught at least two week-long intensive classes. Usually I taught 'Introduction to Islam', 'Spiritual Warfare', and/or 'Discipleship of Leaders', subjects that were required for all students at MTC. John says I came at just the right time because I soon replaced someone who was unable to continue teaching 'Spiritual Warfare'. God's timing is always perfect!

---

[32] Now Lee University, Cleveland, Tennessee.

For the discipleship course I used the book, *Disciples Are Made Not Born*.[33] For the spirituality course I used, *Mighty Prevailing Prayer*.[34] After I visited, seeing the program and meeting the students, I went often and taught for them. I wasn't a 'regular' part of the program (that is, I was not a salaried lecturer), but I loved the school. I went back twice a year at the beginning. In later years, when I became less able physically, I went once a year.

I taught also at the *Faculdade Teologia Evang da Igriga de Deus* (FATEID), in Goiania, Brazil. This school is the superintendent's theological seminary for the country of Brazil. In Ecuador I taught at *Seminario Sudamericano* (SEMISUD) Seminary. I would fly in and out of São Paulo to many other South American countries, such as Argentina, where I taught church people how to reach their neighbors. In the fall I would usually go to Colombia, Venezuela, and Peru. I'd make another circuit to northern Ecuador, then go to southwest to Chile and Brazil during the same time period.

I was enthralled by the beauty I found in South America. For example, the flowers of Brazil were so beautiful. The bougainvillea reminded me of the bougainvillea in Aboud that grew over the top of the church. I always delighted in the poinsettias also, which grew as tall as trees.

Too Much Grief

One time when I was in Venezuela, I was lying in bed and suddenly I saw a vision. I saw a certain man in Cleveland, Tennessee, an official in the Church of God. This man's wife had died.

People ask me, 'You actually feel what they are feeling?' It is awful when you feel the intensity of what someone is going through. Yes, it was terrible to feel that official's hurt and his grief. I had seen that official in a vision pacing the floor in his house and I saw the grief he was suffering. The Lord told me, 'You are to write to him and tell him what you have seen, and that he is grieving too much'.

When I wrote to the official I was to tell him what to do. 'How should I go about it?' I asked, 'What am I to tell him?'

---

[33] Walter Henricksen. *Disciples Are Made Not Born* (Colorado Springs, CO: David C. Cook, 1974, 1988).

[34] Wesley L. Duewel. *Mighty Prevailing Prayer: Experiencing the Power of Answered Prayer* (Grand Rapids, MI: F. Asbury Press, 1990).

'You are to tell him he's to do an "about-face".'

Now, mind you, being a single woman, I'm very careful about contacting a minister who has just lost his wife. I thought, 'Lord, I don't even know if he has an office in Cleveland, Tennessee. I don't know to whom to write or how to get a letter to him.' Then I thought about someone[35] who could probably get the letter to him. I knew she was in Cleveland; and if he had an office there, she would know where he was. So, I wrote her and enclosed the letter for the official. In the note I sent it to her I said, 'I want you to take this letter to him. I don't want you to give it to anyone else.' And she did what I said.

Later, I was telling someone else on the mission field about this experience and that missionary looked at me and said, 'How do you know she won't tell anybody else about this man?'

I said, 'She will do what I asked her to do and then she will forget it'.

When I came home on furlough, I asked my friend, 'By the way, did you give that letter to *so and so*?'

'What letter?' When I reminded her of the details, she remembered it, and I knew she hadn't told anyone.

'Oh yes, I handed it to him personally', she said.

After I returned to Cleveland, I went one day to the Cracker Barrel restaurant to eat. As I was waiting to be seated, that very same official and his new, dear wife came walking out. People were greeting and talking with her. At first, he just stood there, apparently not recognizing me. So I walked over to where he was, held out my hand and said, 'I'm Arlene Miller'.

He immediately said, 'I want you to know your letter came at just the right time. You cannot imagine how I was feeling. When you told me to do an "about face" that really hit. It touched my heart.'

I guessed it did – he got married again!

---

[35] Janice McClung has always been a strong supporter of missions and missionaries. She and Dr Grant McClung have headed the World Christian Prayer Group at Westmore Church of God, Cleveland, Tennessee, for at least 30 years. She is the one, also, who told this writer about Arlene's being in the Meadowbrook Care Center.

Visiting Churches

I visited with the churches in South America when school was not in session, during summer in the southern hemisphere. Mid-November through January I was in Chile where I stayed with Israel and Debbie Minay. The Minays were so wonderful to me. We became good friends. Debbie interpreted for me in Chile and then Giselle Candia took over the task. (Giselle accepted the Lord as her Savior when she attended one of my courses). The Candia family took me in and made me feel like one of their kids, even though I was older than they were.

Do you remember the Russell Stover's candy from the beginning of my story? Debbie was lying on her bed as I was telling her the mushroom story and other stories one evening. She pulled out some chocolate from behind her. Tourists had brought this brand of candy to her, but she said her husband didn't like the dark, chocolate-covered, caramel ones. She asked if I wanted them. Did I want them? YES! (I still get boxes of those chocolates from people and it's been over nine years since I came into this nursing home.)

It was difficult for me not to have a home-base in South America. I would wake up and ask myself – not what city was I in, but what country was I in? I was really moving from country to country all the time.

Arabs In South America

I think knowing that there were many Palestinian Arabs living in South America helped me to feel at home. Everywhere I went in South America I continued to be an evangelist – in Colombia, Ecuador, and elsewhere. Sometimes I would go to the mosque and sit in the foyer and talk with the people. For these men, talking to someone who knew about their country and knew interesting things, like how they make soap out of olives in Nablus (one of the cities they knew in Israel) was like meeting someone from their home country. Though I certainly couldn't talk overtly with them in the mosque about my beliefs, they knew I was a Christian and my 'caring witness' probably opened a door for someone else later. It was important to me to just spend time with them – witnessing, not with words, but just how I treated them. I always tried to make myself available for God to use.

One of the things that intrigued me was why Arabs would have come to South America in the first place. I soon discovered that most Arabs arrived in South America during times of hardship. For example, it was when the Israelis took over Arab homes in Jaffa that the Christian Arabs migrated to Chile.

In each city I visited I would do a 'survey'. Many shops had Arab names. In fact, there were Arabs living across the street from the MTC (Missionary Training Center). I would walk up to them and start speaking in Arabic. They couldn't believe that a North American was speaking in Arabic. Right away they wanted me to say their creed, the *Shahada*, 'there is no God but Allah, and Muhammad is his prophet'. I'd say, 'No I can't say that because I really know Jesus'. Nevertheless, they would invite me to their homes, to their weddings, and to special events. They are the most hospitable people that I have ever seen. Arabs in South America would often grab my hand and take me into their homes and shops. They would immediately want to give me some coffee or candy. Everywhere I went I would go out and establish friendships with Muslim families. I would go to their homes, eat with them, talk with them, and become friends with them. I never tried to learn Portuguese or Spanish. Instead, I kept looking up Muslim families, practicing my Arabic. I 'came alive' when I visited these families who sincerely loved me. Some became Christians. They all loved me and looked forward to my coming every time I was in their city.

It was a time when Muslim influence was growing in South America. Entire neighborhoods were becoming Muslim. There is now an Arab mosque even in São Paulo. I also found that some of our South American overseers were descendants of people from the Middle East. I prayed for them and still do.

Then there were special times. I remember one time in Santiago, Chile: the church had bought a beautiful old synagogue to use as a place of worship. When I walked in, I saw the Star of David covering the ceiling and I thought to myself, 'They'll never get an Arab inside'. I knew that even the Christian Arabs have a hard time dealing with the Star of David.

A Christian Arab woman came up to me after worship in that church, however, and she asked, 'Do you speak Arabic?' It turned out that she'd attended that church for years, and we became great friends. The Star didn't seem to distract her. Her name was Ilene. She would invite me to her house for a meal of good Arab food: grape leaves and rice. Of course, she also had little silver-plated nut dishes with all kinds of seeds in them: watermelon and pumpkin seeds, which had been roasted with salt and were called *bizer*.

When teachers from the USA would come to moderate retreats to very special places, the Arab Christians included me and never charged me an entry fee – even though an entry fee was often required. I did a chaplaincy course at a Catholic retreat center on the seacoast of Chile. They made me feel so welcome.

Training Missionaries

During the time I was in South America I was involved in training more than 100 Latin Americans in cross-cultural ministry. I had the privilege of helping prepare missionaries to do ministry in various continents. I am thankful that many Church of God South American missionaries are now entirely supported by South American church members. I had an opportunity to interact with church leaders at regional and national levels: missions mobilizers, leaders, and church planters. I discovered there were many with a heart for reaching new cities as pioneer church planters all over South America. My emphasis, of course, was to challenge them to reach out to Muslims. We had the privilege of helping prepare Lee interns from the USA for missions – over 50 have been trained and encouraged to reach Muslims. We helped prepare missionaries from other denominations as well.

I suppose Chile was my favorite country. If you ask me why, it's probably because of all their college-educated young people who spoke a lot of English. They invited a few adults like myself to parties, though they said they usually didn't invite adults. I reminded them that I was an adult, too! My hosts there were so special – especially, the Minays. Debbie and Israel were very gracious. I traveled with his father, José Minay, too. I just felt at home with them. When I visited, José would go buy German cheesecake, a favorite of mine. When he was there, we had fresh bread all the time. He would go out early in the morning and bring it in. They are such a wonderful family with very well-behaved kids.

In Chile there is a spectacular natural stone gateway standing out in the ocean. Giselle's father took a picture of it when I was staying with them. It hangs in my room today.

Interpreters

Interpreters were an important key to my ministry. Sometimes John Hayes interpreted, but I also used several other interpreters. I enjoyed my relationships with my interpreters and other faculty members.

In the South American Seminary (SEMISUD) in Quito, Ecuador, David Ramírez and Pablo were a great help to me. In northern Chile, I'd stay with Giselle, my interpreter, at her home in Anta Fagusta. Gisele interpreted for me in Santiago, Chile.

In Argentina, Rev. Osvaldo Pupillo and his family were always so hospitable, asking what I would like, and preparing special meals for me. I think my interpreters were the very best. In addition to Giselle in Chile, and Pablo in SEMISUD, there were Josue Candido and Sueli Felipe in Brazil, and Sausto in Venezuela, who even came once to Chile to be my interpreter – maybe the Minays were on furlough at that time. They were always so hospitable! Of course, in Argentina, the steak was incredible.

Many people told me that using an interpreter is not the best method to teach lessons or preach sermons. Someone (at one of the largest black churches in the USA for the Church of God) told me, however, that my interpreters had the gift of knowing exactly where I was headed in my teaching or preaching. I think he was right.

Giselle interpreting for Arlene.

One time my students said 'Arlene, if you sneeze, Pablo will sneeze, too'. That's the way it was. One of my interpreters, Josue, was a pastor from another denomination who made many missions trips to Mozambique. He even came to Ohio to visit me. I became very close to my interpreters, realizing they were crucial to conveying my message.

It was exciting to watch my interpreters when I preached a special sermon that I called, 'The Arab Bride'. The congregation would be one step ahead of me because they saw where I was going; and the people would be so excited and happy. Josue, the interpreter, was tickled. In the sermon I would compare the coming of the Arab bridegroom with the coming of Christ to his Bride, the Church. There are so many similarities. For example, when he comes, the Arab groom doesn't receive anyone but only the one with the bride's dress on. I could see that they were going to go home and preach that sermon![36]

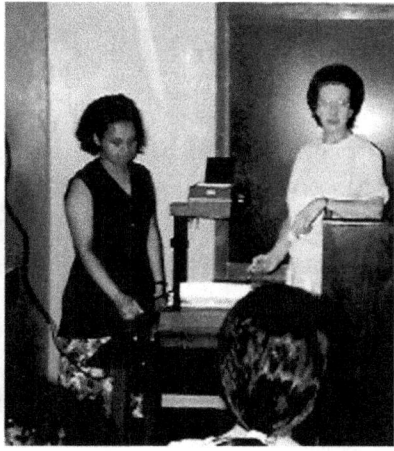

Josue and Sueli in Brazil interpreting for Arlene

Encouraging Young Women

Young women often responded well to me. I visited a small church in São Paulo where I told my testimony and preached about missions. Marie, married to Nivaldo Riveiro, heard me speak, and it touched her heart. She told her husband, 'We have to go study at that seminary'. They got their theological degrees, then they came to the Missionary Training Center (MTC) because of my sharing about missions in that local church. The Riveiros went to Guatemala for one year of service, then they served for eight years in Mozambique, training leaders for their church. They now serve as Coordinators for

---

[36] I heard stories about her telling about an Arab wedding in churches in Ohio, too, and people were blessed to now understand that He 'has gone to prepare a place for us!'

the Missionary Training Center in São Paulo, which trains missionaries from all over South America. God gave me such wonderful opportunities.

I was particularly drawn to encourage young women to go on missions whether they had a husband or not. I didn't particularly like being single, but I wanted my life to be an example for all those young girls – many of whom are still serving overseas. I had opportunities to meet and encourage young women, not just at the Center, but also at missions' conferences and at many other events. I believe wherever I went I influenced young women to dare to be missionaries.

Relating to Students

I liked being involved with my students. When I lectured, if they dropped a pencil, they would miss taking a whole page of notes! But, I wanted to be open to the Spirit and often we paused for prayer, or for counseling, or for whatever was needed. I frequently spent time with students, talking with them, counseling with them, etc. At MTC I actually lived with the students. There I had a simple room with a table, a bed, and a wardrobe,[37] and I shared a bathroom with the students.

The students and I enjoyed Friday evening meals. As you can read in Appendix G, the center was very concerned about helping the students gain cultural orientation for the places where they were preparing to serve as missionaries. To fulfill this goal, each Friday the students experienced different cross-cultural foods. For example, they would prepare an Arab meal with the help of Arabs in the community who would teach them how to prepare their food. At another time, John's family and I might prepare a North American meal. These were wonderful hands-on learning experiences.

Part of the MTC cultural preparation had to do with other very practical experiences. For example, they might shut the water off for three days! The students and I were allowed to struggle through that challenge together! This was a good way to check students' attitudes and motivation. You see, the Center offered more than academic

---

[37] A wardrobe is a self-standing, portable closet used for the hanging of clothes in a room that has no built-in closets.

training. They brought in professors on a modular[38] basis: the very best teachers in every area. These teachers had to be involved in cross-cultural ministry and in character and spiritual development. They confronted students with the reality of missionary life. Training was very intensive. Teachers lived with the students for three months, like a family living together.

The training center did a complete evaluation on each student with a recommendation, which was given to their overseers and educational directors. Often, I was asked to discern attitudes, the heart and the character of students, so they would be better prepared for the mission field. I was happy to help because I was very concerned that missionaries be adequately prepared for service. Even Lee University used MTC's example to evaluate their missions students. It was very intensive and comprehensive. Faculty came not just to teach the classes but to be involved in the whole learning process.[39]

My students were such a blessing to me. I'd like you to meet some of them: there was Vanessa Lazarte. She really got excited about missions and traveled on several missions trips. When the Lord was dealing with her regarding Muslim ministry at MTC she would sit during my lectures and cry as I taught. She didn't want to, but she knew she had to go to the Muslims. She would just throw up her hands and begin to weep. The other students knew what she was struggling with because she would talk to them after class. 'I just know it's going to be so hard', she would say. As she became full of conviction by the Spirit, she would raise both hands, then bring them down on her desk, weeping loudly. She said, 'I'm going to have to go, and I know it's going to be very difficult work. I can't take any more. I can't take any more.'

That was Vanessa. She said she would be the next Arlene Miller of the Church of God in South America; but unlike me, she did marry! Vanessa and her husband, Alexander Hernández, from Guatemala, were sent to France by the Church of God in Argentina for

---

[38] Teachers came for short courses – perhaps a week or two – to teach a particular course, rather than be in residence for a whole term.

[39] Since his return to the USA eight years ago, John Hayes has traveled back to Brazil – to Manaus on the Amazon River – where he has developed the Arrowhead Project to evangelize, plant churches, and train leaders among the tribal people. Every January he also returns to Brazil to teach at the Missionary Training Center. Meanwhile, he pastors a church in San Jose, California, which he is eager to develop as an international church.

several years, 2007-2009. Vanessa continues to travel to Europe, Asia and the USA, working with the pastoral care of missionaries. Vanessa and her husband now live in Buenos Aires. Vanessa is the Regional Missions Director, taking youth on short-term missions experiences. She also is a representative of EIMI (Agencia de Enlace Misionero Internacional), the Latin American Mission Agency with the Church of God.

Santa 'Teresa' Mamani from Chile was another who had a definite interest in Muslims. She went to India in 2004 and married Samuel Dhanasekaris, an Indian pastor, and still ministers there until today, leading an orphanage and training leaders by initiating a Bible School program.[40]

Teresa, one of Arlene's 'daughters'.

Maria 'Celia' Mendez dos Santos went to Mozambique in Africa in 2003. Since then she has been working with Iris Ministries (under Heidi Baker, CEO) in the orphanage and with the Church of God in establishing pastoral training. She is still single and has had a very successful life and ministry among Portuguese-speaking people in Africa. Currently she is involved with the Church of God World Missions Firewall Project to plant churches in Africa.

Gustavo José Chavez from Argentine was my student and he and Mariani, his wife went to Spain to minister to Muslims for 12 years. He is currently the leader of the Church of God Latin American Missions Board (AEMI). They also pastor a local church in São Paulo.

Patricia Paredes served in Ceuta, Spain, for three months reaching out to Muslims. She married David, has two children, and is now in Iquique, Chile where they have the opportunity to meet a variety of

---

[40] See the Foreword.

people not only from Central and South America but Pakistan and Israel as well. She continues to minister remembering what I taught her about loving Muslims.

In Appendix F you can find a list of several of the graduates with whom I worked. This list is just a representative number. There are many more. The following is a newsletter from that period in which I mention several of the students by name.

Arlene Miller
February, 2004
Project No. #060-0070
... and underneath are the everlasting arms.
Deut. 33.27

Dear Friends,
While in the States at Christmas time, I was involved in an auto accident. On a very slippery, snowy night a car hurtling and sliding broad sided down a steep hill and hit the entire front of my car. From several feet away the car could be seen coming so there was time for me to pull to the right as far as possible and almost be at a standstill. I held the brake and waited. My car was totaled but hardly moved. The other car was knocked across the ditch and up an embankment. I was able to walk away, thank God. The air bag hit me so hard it damaged my right ear. Until now there has been a problem with vertigo because of this. The particles dangling inside the ear make a strange sound with every slight vibration. Most likely a visit to a neurologist will be made when I am back in the States. God's everlasting arms do hold us up! Thanks so much for the emails, calls and prayers during the month I was recovering from the impact of the air bag.

Chile The last weekend I spent in Chile was one of the most blessed and precious times to me. Those who know me well know how much I love the young violinist who is the concert master for the national chamber orchestra. Many know some of his story: how he had drifted so far from God and what kind of life he had been living. Over the years so many prayers have been sent up and tears shed concerning his soul's condition. A year ago it was obvious he was struggling and attempting to come back to the Lord.

This time when I got to Chile and he and his wife walked into my room I knew he had more peace than last year. Giselle, my interpreter and I got to be with him several times while in Santiago. His pastor invited me to preach at their church the last Sunday I was in the country. Oh, my. The Holy Spirit moved in such a sweet and blessed way. Many filled the altars. Some were saved while others were filled with the Holy Spirit: I do not know when I have felt the presence of the Lord as much as we did that night. It was impossible to know what to do. Should I walk from one person to another just praying, smiling and praising God or should I fall on my face and just weep? I looked out at the congregation and saw my friend with his hands raised, eyes looking upward, a big smile on his face and praising God. It brought back memories of former years when he had been such a dynamic worship leader. Then I did just walk back and forth smiling, weeping and praising God out of sheer gratitude and joy. God is faithful. If we can just hold on and be faithful in our loving, caring and praying, the victory will come.

Brazil I am back at our WEAC center in São Paulo. Our students this year are from Argentina and Brazil. I shall write more about them in the next letter.

Prayer Requests
Celia was a student here at WEAC last year. She has been in Mozambique now almost a year. We have received great reports from her supervisor about the work she is doing there. She does need your prayers.

Agnoldo came home for a visit in January. He has now been in Mozambique almost two years. He asks that you pray for God to give him a wife who will be a blessing in the ministry with him. He really needs help and wants to be sure he gets someone who will not be a hindrance. This is very important.

Gustavo and Mariani are working hard near Barcelona, Spain. It is difficult for them to understand why the Spanish Christians will not reach out to the Muslim Arabs in their city. We need to pray that God will awaken all Christians everywhere and make them more concerned about the Muslim world.

Dear friends, thank you so much for you prayers and your support. I do feel your prayers and depend upon them. Because of you many more are getting to hear the Words of Life. Soon we shall send our first student to India. Thanks to you for helping to support me so that I may be able to help train many of these workers. Keep those prayers going up.

In Him, Arlene

P.S. I am using a computer that is programmed for Spanish and I cannot find any of the punctuation marks I need.

Education Directors and Overseers

When I went to the schools, most of the time the education directors would host me in their homes because I was a guest teacher. By staying in their homes, traveling with them to meetings with overseers and education directors, I hopefully helped change their attitudes about missions. Most of the problems in mobilizing missions awareness in South America had been with overseers who were indifferent to missions. I saw my personal contact with them as being very important in helping them see their role in mobilizing missions. They sometimes didn't like losing good workers who were attracted to missions, and it was often challenging to encourage them to be good supporters of missions. I believe I helped encourage them to change that perception.

Health Issues

Many times I was sick with my bile-duct problem. I had a hard time. Sometimes, the week before I was going to teach, I would be so ill I could hardly walk; but every time God was able to give me strength to pull through once the class started. Once, in Chile, I passed out in a bathroom and hit my face on the sink. The people were scared to death; but, I told them, 'Just leave me alone and I'll be ok'. In no time at all my face looked a purple mess around one eye. Any time I would be outside in the sun I always had to wear big sunglasses that fit over my regular glasses. When I got in the taxi to go downtown to the seminary, I put on the black glasses to cover my big black eye. I left them on when I entered the building. I even kept them on when I got up in front of the class.

I asked a question: 'How many of you know beyond a shadow of a doubt you are called to the Muslim world?' Every hand in the class went up. I then reached up and took my glasses off and they saw my eye and my cheek and how black and blue it was. I said, 'So, this is your fault because the Devil tries in every way he can to stop me in a place where people are really and truly called to the Muslim world'. The class just roared with laughter.

Every time my interpreters and I would encounter extra trouble we knew that the place we were getting ready to go to would have a lot of students who were definitely called to the Muslim world. One time we got on a plane and the door wouldn't shut. Fausto (my interpreter) and I just looked at one another. I said, 'Well, I wonder what else is going to happen. Wouldn't the Devil have just loved that, if they had not caught that problem when we were on the ground and the door had come open while we were in flight?'

Another time just before we got to the place where we were to have the class a horrible storm came through and destroyed all of the sound equipment. Again, we just smiled, because we knew the Devil was trying to stop us because there were many people there called to the Muslim world.

Many episodes were like that: I would get dizzy and pass out, but somehow, I kept on going. God gave me such strength to persevere, to travel to many places – even though it was not easy to travel in South America and to adapt to new situations. I loved to teach so much! I never doubted but that I could continue traveling and teaching. John Hayes said, 'I don't know how you kept going as you did'. I kept a very busy schedule.

John Hayes

John didn't know my situation or realize that I was grieving until years later, but he understood that grieving is often a long process, especially without pastoral care. Though I was grieving, I didn't burden others with what I was going through – I was focused on the ministry. I was always upbeat and really excited about training the Latin Americans in Muslim ministries.

Years later, I talked to John about my grief; he understood what I was going through because he had been training 'MKs' (missionary kids) who are often called 'Third Culture Kids'. The re-entry process for them is also often very difficult. A lot of that applied to himself and to me also. He had been helped by people like Dave Pollock and Marjorie Foyle as a missionary to understand the cross-cultural process. He understood that leaving Aboud so abruptly was a difficult process for me. He felt that – like the Muslims described by Dr Douglas – that I, too, had been overlooked by many and not appreciated.[41] He thought that though I was very important in the teaching and administration of the school in Aboud, I was seldom mentioned. At one point I talked to him about how we had to fight to keep that school open when, unfortunately, it's worth was being considered in terms of investment or money. He understood our heart for the school and for the Arab people. John is such a caring and gentle person, I don't think I could have survived in South America without his understanding and support.

My 'Samuel' Circuit

The pattern was the same every year. Like Samuel in the Bible, I made a circuit, coming back home to the USA in the summer. Some of the countries I taught in were Venezuela, Colombia, Peru, Argentina, and Paraguay. Usually I traveled by air, but I remember taking a very hot bus ride from Paraguay to Argentina at least once. I would then fly home to the states for the summer.

John Hayes interpreting for Arlene in Brazil.

During three summers, I went back to attend Bethel Bible College in Springfield, Missouri, under the Zwemer Institute. I also studied

---

[41] See appendix A.

at the Ontario Theological Seminary in Toronto, Canada. After those early years of training, I was home in between itineration appointments during the summer. The Lord had provided my mobile home, but, as you may recall, it was rented out, and I needed to stay with my parents. When Sybil, a woman with whom I evangelized in the States, died, she left a little bit of money – about $3,000. Can you believe, I bought a 12' x 60' one-family mobile home with that money? Sybil and I had never had a place to live in when we were evangelizing. We had to store our things in various places. When we were evangelizing, we always said if we ever could afford a trailer, we would get one with bedrooms at either end and a lavatory with two sinks and two mirrors in the middle. The trailer that I bought had bedrooms at either end and a lavatory with two sinks and two mirrors in the middle! God is so good!

When I returned to South America, I would teach the same weeklong intensive every place I went. Students came from Cuba, Argentina, Chile, Brazil, and Paraguay. They were shocked at how similar Islam is to Christianity. Some really felt called minister to Muslims. Some of my students came to the MTC center after I had taught in their churches, but others were already students at the center. My main aim was not to recruit students for the center when I spoke at the churches. I was primarily wanting to teach them how to reach their Muslim neighbors for Christ, but some were certainly called to Muslim work in those churches and did come to the center for preparation.

I traveled as far as the Philippines to teach at the Asian Center for Missions under Miguel Alvarez, President of the Asian Seminary of Christian Ministries. When Dr Alvarez contacted me about teaching in the Philippines, I gave him a preferred date. He said the only date they had open was the week I had purposely left vacant to view the autumn leaves in Ohio. I prayed about it, but I didn't have to pray much. I knew I had to go. Pat Robertson had started a 'sister school' on the same Church of God property as ASCM called the Asian Center for Christian Ministries (ACM). While the first was a seminary, the second was a school for missions. Often the students of ACM had to go as domestic helpers or English teachers to closed countries, but they went secretly to share the Gospel with people.

When I got there, I asked the students how many could have come the next week. None of them! They were leaving to go back to their posts of duty, and some were going back to dangerous assignments like Saudi Arabia. It was well worth it, and I was glad I went.

I even taught discipleship in Oslo, Norway. Although I had been invited, I was still hesitant. They kept asking me if I was going to come to teach and I kept ignoring them, but finally I agreed. When I arrived, they asked if I had prayed about it and I had to admit I hadn't. The people were from Norway but had immigrated to Chile and at that time were returning to Norway. They saw how badly people in their home country needed discipleship. It turned out to be a wonderful week of teaching.

Understanding Muslims

Dr Douglas had taught me that there are many misunderstandings about Muslims.[42] One is that we equate Arab with Muslim, which of course is not the case. There are millions of Muslims who are not Arabs at all. And many Arabs are not Muslim. So, with the 'why' of reaching Muslims clearly in mind, I began my seminars with the history of Islam and its founder, Muhammad. For more information about what I taught see Appendix A.

Reaching Out to Muslims

One of the most important topics which I taught was how to witness to Muslims. Prayer is vital and especially important in establishing relationships with them. I discovered that shopping in their stores and meeting them in informal settings is very important. For Muslims, life is all one piece. You may walk into a Muslim store and often discover they are in the back, kneeling and praying. Don't interrupt them. These prayers, five times a day, are very important to them.

Dr Douglas stressed how important stories are in reaching Muslims. One example he used when discussing the Muslim faith with Muslims has to do with Muhammad and Jesus. Muslims face a dilemma here because Muslims can go to the grave of Muhammad but there is no grave for Jesus. If they do start talking to you about Islam or if you start the conversation, you might then ask, 'Where was

---

[42] See Dr Douglas' article in Appendix A.

Muhammad born? And where was he buried?' The answer is, of course, 'He's in the grave in Medina and you can visit it'.

'Could you visit Jesus' grave?'

'No.'

'Where was Jesus buried? Could you visit his grave?'

'No, he ascended.'

'Well, then if you needed Muhammad to help you, would you visit Muhammad's grave?'

'No.'

'Could you visit Jesus' grave?'

'No.'

'Who could help you now?' [43]

'Jesus, because you could visit his grave, but he is not there, he is alive.'

'Do you want to talk to one who is entombed or to one who is alive and active?' Muslims believe that Jesus did not die, but was 'taken up'. He, therefore, is the one they can talk to.

Another story made the rounds in Cairo. There was a young Muslim man who died. The *imam*[44] was jealous of the American missionary because the people liked him so much. Challenging the missioning, the *imam* went to a big gathering where the people were listening to that missionary. The imam asked, 'You knew Hdakim who died. Where is he today, heaven or hell?'

The American missionary, with the wisdom of the Holy Spirit, answered, 'Did he go to Mecca? Did he pray five times a day? Did he say the *shahada*? Yes? Well then, that's easy. He's with Muhammad.' The people laughed! They thought it was a good answer.

Since Issa (Arabic name of Jesus) is in the Qur'an,[45] you can use the name of Jesus – just don't talk about God the Father, or the Son, or use Jn 3.16. They don't believe Jesus was the Son of God, and they believe strongly that God bore no children.

Evangelism must come out of relationship. You have to be interested in them, and really love them. You need to get to know them well. You can then introduce them to the person of Jesus. They will

---

[43] Arlene credits this insight to Dr Douglas.

[44] *Imam* is used here, in a general sense, as a religious leader. *Imam*, in particular, is the religious leader believed to have succeeded Muhammad.

[45] Islam's holy book.

know if you are loving them and are their friend or if you are just pretending to be their friend in order to convert them.⁴⁶

---

⁴⁶ For more information about how to reach Muslims, see the Appendix section of this book.

10

FINAL REFLECTIONS

What would I want my readers to learn about the Lord from my experience with Him? We may not always understand Him, but he is faithful. It may not seem like it sometimes, and he does not always tell us the 'whys' of life, but he has his reasons and someday we will understand many things that have happened to us. I think if people go through life just looking for the day when they will understand, they need to know it won't be important when this life is over. When we get to heaven, I firmly believe we will not even want to understand – or to be reminded of certain things we went through.

If you ask me about beautiful things, I'd need to mention the beautiful mountains and the Finger of God mountain in Brazil. When I heard I was going to South America, I wondered how I was going to do all the traveling because of finances. I received a letter from some friends in the Dakotas. In the letter they said, 'The Finger of God that points the way is attached to the Hand of God that will supply all of your needs'.

As we were going to a meeting in Brazil, John Hayes said, 'Look to the left and you will see the hand of God'. It was a mountain that looked exactly like a hand pointing the way. When I got to the meeting, I was informed that the main speaker could not come. They asked me to preach all of the sermons. I agreed. At the end of the conference they presented me with a gift. I had told the story about the 'Finger of God'. The gift they gave me was a plate with a picture of the Finger of God mountain on it. I thought it was very apropos because God had supplied my needs. I still have pictures of the Finger of God mountain in my room at the Care Center.[47]

Someone said to me once, 'The fingerprints of God are hard to see – at the time'. This has been so true in my life. Often, I have not understood what God was doing until much later. Since that saying was so important to me, I even had it printed for a professor I knew who was 'jerked' out of his position very abruptly. He, too, said the saying ministered powerfully to him.

People ask me if I have been retired. No, I would have still been working if I'd not broken my neck and suffered severe nerve damage. I would certainly have continued.

While in South America, I didn't speak the language (except through an interpreter). I often felt very alone. I didn't really have someone to talk to like my grandmother had talked with me. How did God sustain me during that lonely time? Like he always did – he has always been 'just there'. I don't know what I'll do tomorrow, but I know he is with me *today*.

There were special times that I remember. I especially loved when the first-chair violinist, Hernon Julio, would bring several members of the national chamber orchestra of Chile to the Minays' church to do a concert every year. He was a wonderful worship leader in one of the churches in Santiago. As a minister himself, he had a great respect for most ministers. He believed that they should be supported very well, as they were worth it. He treated me like a queen, taking me and my interpreter, Giselle, to concerts where he was playing, seating us in those nice theatre boxes. Afterward we would go out to eat. He would always take us to the nicest restaurants. He always carried his violin with him – even into the restaurant – because one time he had one stolen from him.

---

[47] This is the cover picture. The idea of the 'finger of God' comes originally from Scripture in Exod. 31.18 where it describes how God wrote the Ten Commandments. Jesus proclaimed himself God as he wrote on the ground with his finger in Jn 8.6. It was immortalized in Michelangelo's painting in the Sistine Chapel that portrays the creation of man. The mountain pictured on this plate which hung in Arlene's room is located an hour and a half outside of Rio de Janeiro near the city of Teresópolis. Donald McGavran used this expression to indicate how God prepares peoples and populations for receptivity to the Gospel when he said, 'The time is ripe. God is now pointing his finger at the most responsive world believing Christians have ever contemplated' ('A Giant Step in Christian Mission,' *Mission Frontiers*, January 1, 1986). Surely, it was also the 'finger of God' that pointed the way for me to enter Arlene's room and become part of her wonderful story.

One day Julio slipped something into my suit-jacket pocket. I asked him what he put in my pocket. Knowing him, he would sometimes stick a french fry into it; this time it was a $100 bill!

The fingerprints of God are sometimes hard to see, but the LORD was showing me, 'God sees you, and he cares for you'. He holds me up. Even when I don't see him, the fingerprints are there. His fingerprints appear differently for each person, but they are surely there.

Hernon Julio with Arlene – musician and friend

When I was back in the USA, I would visit many churches. I've observed that Americans are often very ignorant and don't know where the rest of the world is, but they are good-hearted. One time, Earl Brown, then overseer of Michigan, invited me to give a seminar at a Dearborn, Michigan, church pastored by Pastor Fred Nichols. When Earl asked me to give a seminar, I told him I would present that week-long seminar if he would arrange for me to speak in five churches before the seminar.

'Why?' he asked.

'Because the whole world wants to reach the Jews, but no one cares about the Muslims', I responded.

I'm excited that Fred and Melody Nichols are now going to Europe to reach Muslims.[48]

---

[48] When I asked Arlene what advice she would give the Nichols as they launch forth into Europe, she said she would give them her notes! Actually, the Nichols have worked for many years in outreach to Muslims in Dearborn, Michigan, which

One of the saddest things to me was to see other missionaries that I knew, like John Hayes, who had to return from the mission field because of lack of support. As a result of his work in South America, we have many people ministering to Muslims all over the world: in France, in Spain, in India. May God raise up more who will send missionaries to Muslims!

When I look back on my life, I think that God does special things for people who live and work in places that are considered spiritual deserts, like the West Bank in Israel. Why do I say spiritual deserts? Spiritual deserts are difficult places to bring people to the point of conversion. In fact, there is a strong prohibition against such conversions to take place. In those places, the Lord compensates in special ways to keep us from discouragement.

Besides the chocolates and morel mushrooms, there were many times when God just surprised us with something small. I remember my co-worker, Margaret, saying, 'I'm almost afraid to think of something because I almost invariably get it'. For example, she had wanted to attend a servicemen's retreat in Europe and sure enough, the servicemen sent her the money to make that trip.

As for me, I'd depended on Margaret's car for transportation for years; but often, she would be off in Bethlehem and a need would arise. You may not know how much a car would cost in Israel, but it was prohibitive – twice as much as in the United States due to duties and transportation costs from Germany. The Lord provided a Jetta car for me which made it possible for us to take more people to the doctor and to the hospital. I was so grateful for that provision.

Then there was perfume. We couldn't afford extra perfumes. I always put on cologne as the finishing part of dressing. One day I commented to Margaret that I had used the last of my cologne. Sure enough, when an Arab came back to visit his parents, he not only brought presents for them; but also, he brought me cologne – just the kind I liked: *Charlie*. We would have rather seen revival and many

---

has seen a great influx of Muslims in recent years and in many other places in the USA. At present they are organizing, with Sean O'Neal, the first Iranian church for the denomination in California. They have taken the lead in training people how to reach Muslims for Christ. The plan is to make the move to Europe in the fall of 2020 where they will be working in the Muslim world at large – including Europe, the USA, and North Africa.

people coming to receive the Lord; but by providing these little things, God let us know that we were doing what he wanted us to do.

There were so many special kindnesses. God gave us wonderful overseers who always included us in their Christmas celebrations: the Greiners, the Kielweins, and the Schmidgalls.

When Marcia asked me what I would tell a young woman preparing to go on the mission field, I said I would tell her to learn how to sacrifice. You'd be surprised at the number of people who apply to the Mission Board, asking for a swimming pool and a salary far greater than what the people they are going to serve could earn. I would tell her any sacrifice that she will make will be more than compensated for by the Lord. There is such satisfaction in knowing you are doing what God wants. Nothing can satisfy like that does.

Most places in which a missionary goes to serve, those people just assume that you are a rich American or German; however, nothing can convince them that you aren't. Therefore, you will need to prove yourself to them – prove that you really do love the people. They then will understand that although you may have certain things that they do not have; you will use those things to help them.

Arabs knew not to come to us and ask for money. We wouldn't give it to them. We didn't give Bibles away either. We figured if they could buy cigarettes, they could buy a Bible; so we even charged them a small amount for a Bible. We didn't want to cheapen the Scriptures. The Word of God is precious.

A young woman missionary in the Middle East especially needs to be willing to lay down her life, because it is particularly difficult for an unmarried woman to be accepted in that kind of community. They believe that a tree that doesn't bear fruit should be cut down, right? One time a young Muslim man (not our student) threw eggs on our car. The Muslim men chastised him and said, 'Tsk, tsk, it should never have happened to those women'. We had earned their respect because of our sacrificial living.

The apostle Paul is one of the biblical writers that I admire the most. I suppose if given the chance, my question to him would be, 'Did they "bug" you a lot about being single?'

Arabs always thought we were Zionist[49] supporters – and remember, they hated the Jews. One time we had a heavy olive crop. Our teachers couldn't help us care for and harvest the olives. The schoolboys were helping their parents with their crops. We actually gave days off for our students to help their families to pick olives. Margaret was up in an olive tree and I was on the ground picking up the olives. Some Muslim women stood by, ridiculing us. 'Look! They came all the way from America to pick olives.' Ridicule is something that can be expected. If you are single, obey God, walk with him, and don't try to explain to people when they mock you.

I found much more freedom as a single woman in South America, where I even preached in Southern Baptist churches where women are not supposed to preach – but missionaries preach. That's what missionaries do.

Intercessors were very important in our work. Many times, especially when violence loomed, we were aware that people at home were praying for us, particularly at dangerous times when there were demonstrations, etc. Supporters would write and say that they felt led to pray for us at a certain day or time. Sometimes the answered prayer was something simple, reminding us of something we had forgotten, or sometimes the answered prayer was a bigger, more dramatic thing. We found that the Lord is so faithful!

Most of our supporters were from North Carolina, Tennessee, West Virginia, and Ohio. Some I've never met. They must have heard about us through the denominational missions representatives.[50] When one missions representative came to Jerusalem, he visited the overseer. The overseer reported to us that the representative was asked by a minister in the USA about our support.

The representative said, 'I told that minister, "Margaret – she will go visit a church where there's a little woman who gives only $2 a month. Margaret figures everyone deserves to be visited and anyone who writes to them deserves an answer".'

Usually people gave us $10 or $15 a month. They were faithful supporters.

---

[49] A person who believes in the development and protection of a Jewish nation in what is now Israel.

[50] Representatives. Men and women tasked to raise money for missionaries and special mission projects by Church of God World Missions.

This was the day before computers. Oh, the letters we would write! We never had a computer in Aboud, but later we got a word processor. In Brazil, however, there was a computer that I could use to email people. Many people wrote to us.

There were special people like Virginia Lily, who always remembered my birthday and Christmas with cards. Other missionaries encouraged us, like Frances Arch and Everett and Lillian Bragg.

I always loved to teach Old Testament stories – for both young and old, often with flannelgraph pictures. As I lie here in this bed, however, I meditate on the power of the man who is like a tree in Ps. 1.1-3 and pray that it can be said of me:

> *Blessed is the man*
> *Who walks not in the counsel of the ungodly*
> *Nor stands in the path of sinners,*
> *Nor sits in the seat of the scornful;*
> *But his delight is in the law of the LORD*
> *And in his law he meditates day and night.*
> *He shall be like a tree*
> *Planted by the rivers of water*
> *That brings forth its fruit in its season,*
> *Whose leaf also shall not wither;*
> *And whatever he does shall prosper.* (NKJV)

IN MEMORIAM: ARLENE FRANCES MILLER

June 8, 1940 – August 8, 2019

Full moon, rose pink; gray veils:
Arlene greets Jesus! Friends! (Jerusalemites)!

By Janet G. Metzger, PhD, friend, wife of Dr Robert Douglas

August 14, 2019
Duncanville, Texas

Arlene passed away at the Meadowbrook Care Center, Cincinnati, Ohio, shortly after we finished the manuscript for this book, following a brief hospital stay due to a brain bleed. She is finally at rest with her Savior and we can picture her joy at being freed from a body wracked with much pain and suffering.

A memorial service was held at Turner Funeral Home in Hillsboro, Ohio, on August 21, 2019. Pastor Kimble Zornes led the service with several hymns sung by long-time church friends – the McCleese sisters – including 'Blessed Assurance', 'Heaven', 'When We all Get to Heaven', and 'Amazing Grace'. The obituary was read by Pastor Randy Ballard of Kings' Point Church of God, a generous and long-time supporter of Arlene both in her ministry and throughout her illness. John Hayes, her colleague in South America, and Linda Zornes shared testimonies about Arlene's life, and the following eulogy was read by the author of this book. Letters of appreciation were read from Church of God World Missions, which can be found in the Tribute section of this book, along with others received from people whose lives she has touched. Interment followed at the Sinking Springs cemetery.

EULOGY FOR ARLENE MILLER

By Marcia R. Anderson

As I sat down to write about Arlene for this Memorial Service, I realized that each of us probably knew Arlene at a different time. Most of you probably knew her as a child or as a young woman. Probably none of us here knew her well during the Aboud years in Israel. John Hayes knew her in the South American years, and though she and I met occasionally while she was in Aboud and South America, I suppose I knew her most in the twilight years. Together, today we will remember her and give thanks to God for her life.

When I sit down in the mornings to have my devotions, I remember how we read the Psalms and listened to the wisdom of Oswald Chambers in *My Utmost for His Highest* over the telephone. She would say, 'He really hit it, didn't he?' or 'He got that right'. I believe the Lord sent me to Cincinnati at least in part to be Arlene's friend during the very difficult, painful last years of her life.

I met Arlene at a missions conference in North Carolina where we were both sharing missionary stories. She shared her famous 'chocolate story', about how she expressed her longing for some dark chocolate-covered caramel Russell Stover candies one day to her partner, Margaret Gaines, and how the next day a visitor to Aboud had brought her the very ones she wanted. She loved to remind me that she knew exactly what kind they were before she even opened them.

She saw this as an example of how God loves his missionary daughters and wants to encourage them in small ways to help them keep going.

As I reminisced with Arlene for the book which we wrote together, *The Finger of God in the Muslim World: The Life Story of Missionary Arlene Miller*, she told me that she was born to Frank Oliver Miller and Mary Frances Reed Miller in Highland County at her grandmother's home on June 8, 1940, the first of four sisters: Arlene, Phyllis, Elaine, and Nadine. She told me about her growing up years, how she had met her Savior, Jesus, as a young girl in churches in Highland County, in Sinking Springs, and Carmel, how her maternal grandmother had confided in her often as a teen-ager and always told her, 'Don't question God, he knows what he is doing and he doesn't often answer those "why" questions anyway'. How she had enjoyed her best friend Janet Stultz and her cousins with whom she would enter eating contests centered on that good chicken and noodles or beef and noodles that their aunties made! She told me about the quintet that sang together at church. Though she didn't feel she had any voice left, we did sing 'Amazing Grace' together with her visitors just a couple of weeks ago. She told me about being filled with the Holy Spirit and how Ruth Steele and Sybil Cannon influenced her life and ministry, how they helped nurture in her the gift of discernment and prophecy that was to operate throughout her life.

Arlene had the unique ability to feel what other people were suffering, to know just what to say to them to bring hope and comfort. Even to the very end, people who were suffering and wanting to die were brought to her for a word of encouragement. She would tell them, 'Join the club! I want to die, too, but the Lord hasn't answered that prayer yet!' But now he has, and she is safe in his arms.

Arlene had great faith. When Margaret Gaines wrote and asked her to come to Israel to help her, Arlene bought a ticket and landed in Israel, though Margaret had never corresponded with her again. Her father in incredulity said to her, 'You're going to go but you've never heard again from her?' A couple of near-death accidents occurred about that time and Arlene told her father that if she couldn't walk, he should just put her name on a card around her neck and put her on the plane to Israel. She was determined to go, but Arlene just knew Margaret would be at the airport to meet her plane, and she was.

God had prepared Arlene perfectly to help Margaret, who had no elementary education credentials to head the school. To give her time to prepare, Arlene taught 4-6 grades at the Aboud Elementary School for 10 years before she was officially made the principal. She told me how the children at lunch time would bring pita bread with olive oil and spices on it and were insistent on getting close to her with their oily hands, until she would say, 'Someone is going to be able to eat my clothes with all this oil and spices on them'. She spent 10 more years as the principal, preaching occasionally at the church, also, and teaching Sunday school. Those were wonderful years for Arlene, and she was not prepared to have those years end as suddenly as they did.

Arlene, however, was a minister, and she put the needs of the people she was ministering to ahead of her own. She took some courses with Zwemer Institute for Islamic Studies and at the Pentecostal Theological Seminary to prepare her to go to South America to work with John Hayes – who is here today – at the Missionary Training Center in São Paolo. This specialized training enabled her to travel widely in South America to teach churches how to reach the Arabs and other Muslims in their cities for Christ.

She would still be doing that had it not been for the accident which occurred here in Hillsboro in 2009. Arlene suffered from a bile duct disorder which affected her vagus nerve and subsequently caused her to pass out. That hot summer day, she felt an attack coming on, tried to get help, but fell and broke her neck on the curb, necessitating 12 screws to hold her together. I don't think any of us could have imagined what it would be like to see one's limbs deteriorate to the point where Arlene would be frozen in one position day after day. She had to be cared for like a baby. Arlene had only two sources of contact with the outside world – the telephone which she could use with her left hand and her position facing the door of her room from which she could watch the comings and goings in the nursing home. I think when that second option was removed, due to a roommate who insisted on pulling the curtain between them, that God knew it was time to bring his servant home.

Arlene loved the Psalms. Our book, which will be available both as a paperback and an e-book, ends with this Psalm which she dearly loved:

Blessed is the man
Who walks not in the counsel of the ungodly
Nor stands in the path of sinners,
Nor sits in the seat of the scornful;
But his delight is in the law of the LORD
And in His law he meditates day and night.
He shall be like a tree
Planted by the rivers of water
That brings forth its fruit in its season,
Whose leaf also shall not wither;
And whatever he does shall prosper. (NKJV)

May Arlene rest in peace

TRIBUTES TO ARLENE MILLER

CHURCH OF GOD WORLD MISSIONS
ASSISTANT DIRECTOR

August 12, 2019

To the Family of Sister Arlene Miller

LaQuita and I wish to extend our sincerest condolences to you on the passing of your sister, Arlene. Please know that you are remembered in our prayers. The scriptures remind us that weeping may endure for the night, but joy cometh in the morning. She has now heard the Lord say, "Enter in, my good and faithful servant. Enter in to the joys of the Lord."

Trust in the Lord! God is faithful and sufficient to help you through these next few weeks and months with added comfort and strength. We do have a blessed hope in the Lord, *"For the Lord himself shall descend from heaven with a shout, with the voice of the archangel, and with the trump of God: and the dead in Christ shall rise first: Then we which are alive and remain shall be caught up together with them in the clouds, to meet the Lord in the air: and so shall we ever be with the Lord. Wherefore comfort one another with these words."* 1 Thess. 4: 16-18

On behalf of World Missions, we cherish and honor your sister's sacrificial and fruitful years to the kingdom of God. Please accept our condolences and may you find comfort in my words today. May the grace of God that passes all understanding be with you!

Sincerely,

M. Thomas Propes

M. Thomas Propes, D.D.
Assistant Director of World Missions

MTP:c

Arlene Miller was a Teacher and a Friend.

Arlene was involved for several years teaching English at the Aboud Elementary School. She was engaged with Church of God youth, Sunday school, Bible study and she substituted for Margaret Gaines in the Sunday service. Arlene was the headmistress of Aboud Elementary School from 1983-1993. I was her assistant director.

Arlene Miller dedicated herself to the Lord. She was committed to her calling. Her love and sacrifice for her Saviour made her to overcome the difficulties of a different culture and the struggle of learning a different language that she faced throughout her 20 years in Aboud.

She was faithful, loyal, and trustworthy. She had the spirit of service and cooperation that strengthened her leadership. Her sacrifice and friendship were an example for the Aboud people – especially the youth. so that she left an impact in their lives. She was a friend and teacher for them and for me, too.

Most of all, she loved to teach the Word of God!

Suhaila Khalil Khoury, Director
Aboud Elementary School
Aboud, Israel

The Impact of Arlene Miller

It is very difficult to summarize the impact of Arlene in my life in a just a few lines! God used Arlene so much to influence my life. She taught me to express love for the Muslim Arab peoples – unconditional love, that goes beyond their answers, their culture, and their mistakes. She taught me to wait for the late fruits, or perhaps those that I may never get to enjoy or see in my ephemeral earthly life.

Arlene has been an example in my life of faithfulness, of the love of God, and above all else, of surrender, of self-denial, of going on even with bad health, enduring opposition, persevering when others would have abandoned the mission, and continuing without complaint in the midst of adversity and the ingratitude of some.

Arlene is an example of service, surrender, and commitment. She taught me how to deal with ingratitude from those who do not value or love what God loves, those who only seek their own desires to make a name for themselves. She taught me the virtue of working in anonymity, and also in times where standing and being recognized is a virtue.

I will always remember our talks, the advice and shared dreams and visions of the mission field. I will never forget her teachings when facing a spiritual battle or in discerning and weighing the spirits. Her listening ear and her gift of discernment were gifts from God for her life (which she never admitted to having).

She believed that she has done little for the Kingdom of God and for the extension of his church. Her teachings, her love, and dedication will continue to multiply and grow in the perfect will of the Father. Undoubtedly, God will use all that she left us to continue to bring the children of Ishmael to the knowledge and truth of the Almighty God and his Son Jesus Christ.

We give thanks to God for the life of Arlene Miller. We pray that we will continue the flow of love towards the Arab peoples. May all glory be given to God.

Cristina Lovera de Romera
Minister Exhortador IDD
Missionary among Arab peoples
Salt, SPAIN

Arlene Miller was a Gifted teacher, an Anointed Preacher, a Friend and a Confidant.

She was a God-send to my family in the 1990s when we were ministering in Chile. Our children were young and secretly called her 'Inspector Gadget,' because of the quirky look she wore on her face whenever she left the house in search of anyone who spoke Arabic. Tall, stately in her beige trench coat and uniquely styled sunglasses, Arlene was a sight to behold! We got to know her well during her month-long stays in our home. I am sure my husband and our children can recount the unique influence this special lady had on our lives, but I feel that I was the person most significantly impacted by Arlene.

I served as her official translator during her early years of ministry in Chile. Her life as a missionary touched me deeply. The 'Teacher' in her modeled the joy and importance of preparedness in teaching the Word of God. The 'Preacher' in her demonstrated the value and unique gifting of an anointed woman consecrated to ministry, whether she is single or married.

In retrospect, the counsel I received from her as a friend and confidant were invaluable to my life as a career missionary. I am a witness of the many lives she impacted in Chile. Although she was initially heartbroken and felt displaced by the unexpected re-routing of her missionary trajectory, I am sure she was sent by God to minister in Chile – if not for anyone else, at least for me!

Debbie Minay
Missionary from CHILE to CAMBODIA

A Dedication to My Dear Spiritual Mother:

When I was about 17 years old, I met Sister Arlene Miller in the Church of God in Valparaíso, Chile. She preached about the need to take the gospel to the Muslim people and told us about her life on the mission field in Israel. God impacted my life with her testimony began to create a missions calling in me.

About four years later, Arlene returned to Valparaíso. We then were able to develop a friendship. I went to study at CTM in Brazil the next year and she was one of my professors.

She was my mentor in missions who motivated me to know and love Muslim people groups.

God permitted me to serve in Ceuta, Spain, for about three months and to visit Morocco for a few weeks. I experienced the love of God for the Muslim people in a very real way. I was able to make Muslim friends and to share the gospel with them. Since that time, I have always kept in contact with Arlene through various means. I am now married to David and have two children, Aracel (12) and Joshua (10). When I got married and had my first child, Arlene was able to meet them and she continued to challenge us to be involved in missions.

In 2018, God spoke to my husband David and I, along with our two children to move to the city of Iquique – a city in the northern part of Chile where there are many foreign immigrants – Peruvians, Bolivians, Venezuelans, Colombians, East Indians, Ecuadorians,

Haitians, Palestinians, Pakistanis, and others. I believe that God has a missionary purpose for my family in Iquique.

Arlene Miller was like a spiritual mother to me and I loved her very much. If I could speak something to her, I would say these words: 'I feel blessed and honored to have known you and to have loved you. From the moment I met you, my life was never the same'.

Patrícia Paredes G.
Iquique, Chile

Arlene Miller Impacted My Life at Very Crucial Moments.

I did not have the exact words to thank her as she deserved. Missionary Arlene Miller was not only a professor, but she was also someone who sat at my side during lunch so I could 'practice English,' as she called it. She was the person who encouraged me when she perceived my thoughts about 'not being able to make it'. She was the one who told me to not be afraid when I felt alone because God was with me.

She told me to trust in God when it appeared that nothing would turn out right. She told me on various occasions to listen attentively to the voice of God and to know that he would guide me. In fact, I have a keepsake copy of her last words to me written in a letter, saying: 'I am so glad you came to CTM. I trust and pray that all of your classes that you had here will help you wherever God places you. Listen carefully to Him. Many people will tell you what you should do; but just be sure you hear God's voice and obey it'. (See below). Many years later while serving as a missionary, I still remember her words of encouragement. I have learned to love the people that she taught me to love. Her help and encouragement were very important to me, and I will never forget it. It is with all my affection and all my heart that I thank God for her having impacted my life!'

Alejandra Zamúdio
ARGENTINA/BRAZIL/SENEGAL

Arlene's Letter to Alejandra:

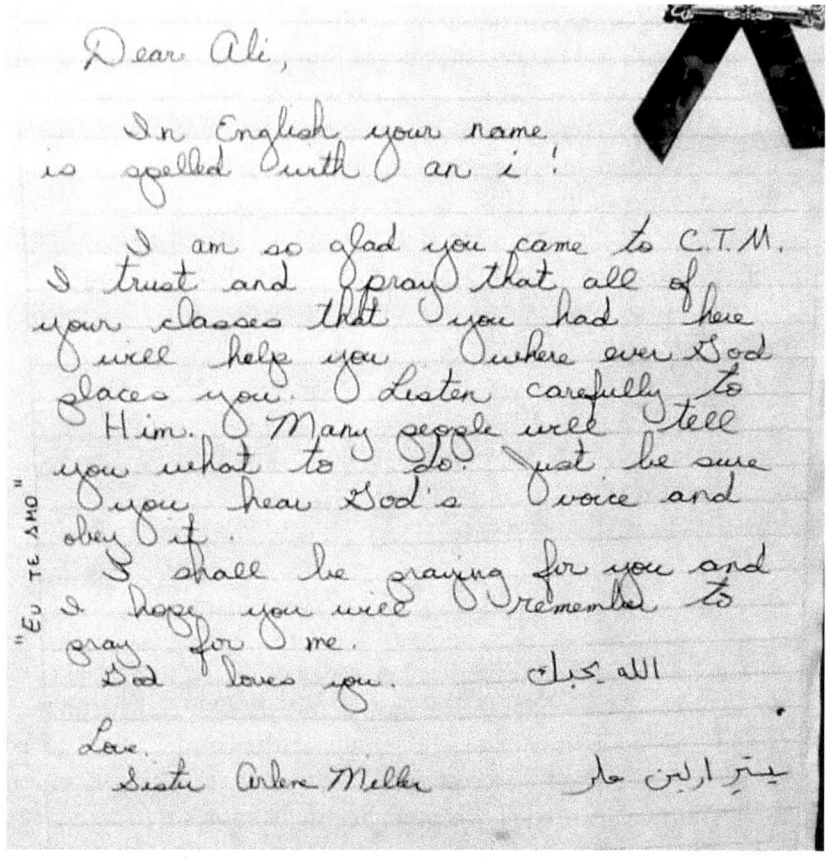

Arlene Miller: A Selfless Servant of God.

Living in Cleveland, Tennessee, I have the privilege of seeing and visiting with missionaries coming through town. When Arlene Miller had been in Cleveland, we scheduled lunch together to catch up on some news. During those lunch times, she would tell me all about happenings in the mission field work. Most of her time would be spent talking about someone the Lord had laid on her heart and how she had been interceding for that one.

Arlene was a unique person in that she had the God-given ability to love nations as well as hurting individuals. Once Arlene was compelled of the Lord to send a letter of instruction and encouragement to a church leader. She asked me to deliver it and I did so. To this day, I cannot remember to whom I took the letter, nor where it was taken. I must stress that Arlene rarely mentioned names when sharing her burdens with me for certain people, but only asked me to pray with her.

We always asked Arlene to come to Westmore's Missions Prayer Meetings when she was in town. She was one of the first people to light the fire of the Holy Ghost in our hearts to intercede for the Muslim world. She had such a fiery compassion and love and concern for a people we were only beginning to know and understand! My friend, Arlene, was one of the most selfless servants of God I know, and I loved her.

> Janice McClung, Chair
> World Christian Prayer Movement
> Westmore Church of God
> Cleveland, Tennessee, USA

A Dedication to My Dear Spiritual Mother.

I remember the first time that I saw Arlene Miller in Santiago, Chile, when I was a student at the Biblical Seminary (2001). I first noted her smile and her simplicity as she taught us the 'Introduction to Islam' course. While she told us about her experiences in the field and all that she had learned, I admired her dedication and ministry as an example of a female missionary, giving up so many comforts to go to a country that was totally foreign to her. Her courage and self-denial were an inspiration for my life.

While she was speaking, my admiration grew for so many really different customs that I was not aware of. She helped me have an idea of how to understand the Muslim people that are also in the heart of God. Since my calling was to India, all that she shared with me was very useful for my future work there. I also learned from her the seriousness of our responsibility as disciples of Christ and how to be a good missionary. When I shared with her about my calling to India, she was very happy because it meant that I could also have the possibility of working among the Muslim people groups. She was so accessible and so open to talk with me. From that very moment on, my heart was attached to hers.

About a year later, I went to Brazil to study at the Missionary Training Center. I had the surprise and joy of seeing her once again. We had the opportunity to share more because she remained longer in Brazil and I could spend more time with her. She motivated me to learn English since it is very important to speak English as a means of communication in India. She influenced me greatly to observe her dedication to the ministry and her sincere love for her beloved people in Israel. She influenced my decision to follow my calling, loving God in the first place and seeking him first. It was the only way for me to understand the heart of God and his love for the nations, tribes, and peoples.

Throughout this time, I was able to get to know a woman that was very caring, simple, and sometimes solitary. She was always happy, however, sharing with us during the moments of relaxation. She did not always have good health, but even so, she tried to spend time with the students at CTM. I give thanks to God because I had the opportunity to study at CTM for nearly two years during which I got to know her very well. I will never forget her encouraging me to learn English. She assisted me by writing the verbs in the past, present, and future tenses. She also taught me the pronunciation of the words. She was more than a friend, for she became a spiritual mother to me, always communicating with me through e-mails. Though she could not be with me physically in India, she was always present through her heart and through her prayers as she was also always in my prayers and in my heart.

More than a missionary, professor, counselor, warrior, etc., Arlene was a woman that served as an example to follow and without doubt left her legacy and mark on many hearts. She challenged many to put their hand to the plow and work with discipline, dedication, and responsibility on the mission field and wherever we were to serve. For those who knew her and those who learned to love her, she will always be a woman who will be impossible to forget. She was a true woman of God, yet still human like the rest of us. For me, she was a mother, and an example to all women.

Teresa Mamani
Missionary from CHILE to INDIA

Arlene's Gift to Me: The Finger-print Picture.

After Arlene had preached at the Carmel, Ohio, Church of God, she gave an altar call. This was the last time I got to hear her preach. She asked us to submit wholeheartedly to the call of God on our lives. As I went forward and was pouring out my heart to God, Arlene came and prayed with me. Afterwards she brought the finger-print picture to me, and said, 'God's fingerprints are all over your life'. She also handed me a note with her phone number. She invited me to call her any time I needed someone to pray or talk with. Those were some rough years for me as my husband had left me alone with three sons to raise. I was never alone. The rejection of the husband of my youth only drove me closer to our Lord and Savior. He will never leave us nor forsake us. I loved hearing Arlene's sermon on us being the 'Bride of Christ'.

Rachel Akers, Member
Carmel Church of God
Carmel, Ohio
USA

APPENDIX A

Zwemer Institute for Muslim Studies

Exactly what was the Zwemer Institute for Muslim Studies where Arlene studied? Dr Robert Douglas says there are many misunderstandings about this. Zwemer Institute is not a Muslim institution nor is it propagating Islam. It is an evangelical, interdenominational organization whose goal is to plant churches among the Muslims. At the time of its founding in 1979 it was the only organization dedicated to that purpose. Of course, this is exactly what MTC wanted to do in South America – teach Christians there how to reach the Muslims and to plant churches among them. The seminars Arlene attended under Dr Robert Douglas and Dr Phil Parshall were very helpful to her as she began to do her own seminars. Like them, she wanted to try to inform people in South America about the needs of Muslims. We also serve churches and organizations in how they might direct their finances and resources to reach Muslims for Christ.

At the time, the Zwemer Institute had already trained 800 missionary candidates or missionaries, like Arlene, who were home on leave. They had also carried out missions work themselves in the Los Angeles area where they reached out to Turks, Iranians, Afghans and others. Some Muslims there had come to the Lord.

Zwemer is the family name of Samuel Zwemer, a pastor of Dutch Reformed Church background who died in 1952. He was viewed as sort of the modern-day apostle to Islam. He functioned in the Persian or Arabic Gulf (depending on your political position) and pioneered from about 1890 to the 1930's in reaching the Muslims. The Institute decided to use his name to remind those in the Institute what they were about and to pick up on the spirit and devotion and commitment that were his as they went out to look at the Muslim world.

Dr Douglas served as the director of Zwemer Institute from 1986-1994. At the time Arlene studied under Zwemer Institute, its offices were located in Pasadena, California, and it was closely associated with the School of World Missions of Fuller Theological

Seminary. As explained in the text, the professors went to various places to teach their students, such as Bethel Bible College in Springfield, Missouri, and at the Summer Institute of Linguistics in Dallas, Texas. It was at those places that Arlene studied. Zwemer Institute for Muslim Studies also migrated for a short time to Fort Wayne, Indiana.

In 2003 Zwemer Institute moved to the seminary at Colombia Bible Institute, now Columbia International University in South Carolina. The Institute is now named Zwemer Center for Muslim Studies.

Zwemer is a major resource and training center for Christians seeking to engage Muslims with the Gospel. More information can be found at www.zwemercenter.com.

Appendix B

An Apologetic for Muslim Ministry

Why is it important that we seek out the Muslims to minister to them? Dr Robert Douglas began to explain the need to reach Muslims in this way:

> In Gen. 17.18 Abraham said, 'O that Ishmael might live before You!' God said, 'Yes, but your wife Sarah will bear you a son, and you will call him Isaac. I will establish my covenant with him.' Isaac would be the child through whom the covenant would be established, but He went on to say in verse 20, 'As for Ishmael, I have heard you; behold, I have blessed him and will make him fruitful and multiply him greatly'.[51]

'I don't know about you,' Dr Douglas says, 'but I resent being forgotten or overlooked. I like to be included and thought of and to participate.' Dr Douglas summarized,

> Many of us feel that way. Those hopes and desires are not always fulfilled. Fortunately, we believe and serve a God who is always aware of us. Hagar discovered that God is a God who sees each and every one of us. From God's perspective none of us is forgotten or ignored.

Dr Douglas reminds us that when we talk about Muslim peoples, we are talking about segments of the world population that have been for a large measure a forgotten people. That's not too surprising because we are talking about a segment of the world's population that would claim some sort of kinship with Abraham's forgotten son, Ishmael. We know a great deal about Isaac and Jacob, about the 12 sons of Jacob who became the fathers of the 12 tribes of Israel. We know a lot about that lineage because of the tensions in the world, and because of the words in the Old Testament. Ishmael was Abraham's

---

[51] This message is a transcript from a March 13, 1987, radio broadcast at Oak Part, Illinois, Calvary Memorial Church by Dr Robert C. Douglas, entitled *Radio Vault: Muslim Awareness*. Used with permission of the speaker.

firstborn son and when God said, 'You are going to have a son through Sarah', Abraham's response to God was, 'Look, I'm satisfied with Ishmael, why don't we just let him be the one?' God says of Ishmael, 'I will, nevertheless, bless him, and I have heard the cry of your heart'.

'Can you list the 12 sons of Ishmael?' Dr Douglas asks. Their names are listed in the Bible in Genesis 25. He is a forgotten son, not occupying center stage in the Bible or in our thoughts about the world. Muslims feel a kinship with Ishmael. The 12 tribes of Ishmael – multitudes of Muslims look to Ishmael as the Jews look to Abraham and Isaac and Jacob. They see in Abraham what it really means to be a Muslim. Some traditions have arisen that Abraham went to Mecca, which is the center of worship for Muslims today. Muslims believe it was Ishmael who was supposed to be sacrificed. At the last minute his life was spared. There is a strong kinship for them with Abraham and Ishmael because of this belief. For most of us, we are not even aware of this.

We suffer from misinformation about Islam or simply from no information. No information and misinformation will produce neglect at best and at worst fear and prejudice. We struggle with this today. We have this forgotten son of Abraham – and this great body of people – who have been forgotten by the church.

We Americans use the words 'Arab' and 'Muslim' as synonymous. All Muslims aren't Arabs. For example, there are more Indonesian Muslims than Arab Muslims. From our perspective Muslim and Arab are almost one and the same. 'Arab' and 'Muslim' and 'terrorist' also become synonymous. There is no more truth to that than the belief that every Irish person is a terrorist. We don't cringe at the thought of Irish neighbors being terrorists. It is not true, also, that all Muslims and Arabs are terrorists.

Through lack of opportunity or neglect, the Muslim world is thrust in our faces and constantly confronts us. You can't pick up the *Chicago Tribune* without finding something from the Muslim world – politically, economically, socially, and spiritually.

Politically

If we had a parliamentary system like Britain, the government would have had to resign in the wake of the Iran Hostage situation. The Muslim world has impinged on us, in the Iran Embassy hostages, hijacked airlines, losing marines in Beirut, the Twin Towers, etc.[52] We struggle with the Muslim world with all of its different dimensions and try to decide foreign policy.

Economically

Louisville, Kentucky, has great horse breeding farms around Lexington that are owned by Muslims. There is farm land in Iowa owned by Muslims. There is also resort land in Florida that is owned by them. While we deeply resent manipulation of the oil market, we all have to admit that we would have pumped Iran and Saudi Arabia dry for a nickel a barrel. We need to understand the resentments we have engendered.

Socially and Spiritually

There is a spiritual impact. Though the census does not reveal religion, it is well known that there are above a quarter-million Muslims in Chicago, a third-million in Los Angeles and two and one half to nine million Muslims in the U.S.[53] Muslims have a determination to proclaim their beliefs to potential converts – to people who can be impacted. Regional training centers operate to train Muslim missionaries for the U.S. Ismael Faruki who taught at Temple University in Philadelphia said, 'We must target 50-70 million Americans to turn to Islam. People are looking for salvation, and we have the salvation they are looking for.' We shouldn't be surprised to discover that there are people representing Islam in the media. The Islamic Center of New Mexico has satellite capabilities ready to reach the whole United States for Islam. They want to reach the world with the 'gospel' of Islam.

The Soviet government wants to placate the Muslims of Central Asia. There are Muslims in Afghanistan, Nigeria, and the Philippines.[54] They are often labeled communist, but Muslims mainly just want to be a part of the economy of these countries.

Why is this being thrust upon us? Is God not simply saying, 'Look Church, you have ignored the Muslim world almost from the outset, and there has been very little done to reach them with the gospel.

---

[52] My update.
[53] These figures are from 1987. There are many more today
[54] During his broadcast message, Dr Douglas stated that the U.S. was not the only place experiencing an upsurge in Islam. He predicted that by the year 2000, 50% of the soldiers in the Soviet Union would be Muslim. The Soviet Union, however, officially broke up in 1991.

You have ignored them long enough, and I will confront you with them, one way or another.' We need to take up the cause and reach out to Muslims.

It is helpful to look at the early Christians. They stayed comfortably in Jerusalem until God brought outside forces to bear on them, so they had to move out. God worked through Cornelius and Peter to confront leaders with the fact that there was a Gentile world. After Acts 13 they moved seriously into Gentile missions. It wasn't a committee doing it nor was there major rethinking. God had the Holy Spirit say, 'Set these people apart for Me' (Acts 13.2).

If there is a task he has for us today, it is to reach the Muslim world. We discover that the church is confronted with one of the greatest challenges ever. We hear a great deal about the dangers of communism and secular humanism. In the two-thirds world, communism is worn out, and the number of active members is small. In relation to the one billion people who see their task and purpose is to preach Islam to the whole world, communism and secular humanism are a bit 'wimpish' by comparison.

If we are not careful, we may lose sight of the challenge of reaching out to Muslims. There is a world out there that God loves and is concerned about. One in five is a Muslim, one in ten is a Muslim woman. Christian women, therefore, have a great role to play because of the sex roles, which make it difficult for men to reach Muslim women.

The sheer numbers are staggering. They are found everywhere on the face of God's earth. Surinam is 25% Muslim, there are one-half million in the Saõ Paolo area of Brazil alone. Albania is at least 65% Muslim. There are 50 million Muslims in the Soviet Union. There are 20 million in China. Thailand has 4 million, and on and on.[55] Of course they are here in the U.S. There is a tremendous geographical spread. We can't say 'a Muslim is a Muslim is a Muslim'. They are diverse: nationally, ethically, linguistically, denominationally, theologically. It is a great challenge!

Islam is an urban religion
Our world is rapidly growing urban. The Christian church for the last 50 years or more has consistently retreated into the suburbs. Islam, however, was born in the cities and lives in the cities.

---

[55] Again, these were the numbers in 1987.

Islam is holistic

Islam deals with every dimension of life. For many, Christianity has traditionally been concerned about the soul – life in the 'bye and bye'. While Islam is concerned with eternal life and heaven, it is also a this-world religion, speaking to every dimension of life.' For example, what is the Christian credit card interest rate? The Islamic interest rate is '0'. They would say, 'Look at the corruption of your society with credit cards charging 20%'. On ecology, nuclear weapons, etc., Islam would have an answer to all of those issues. What does Christianity have to say in all of these different areas?

Islam is widespread

China has approximately 50 million or 80 million Christians, and China is only 5% Christian. In the Muslim world, however, only 1/10,000[th] of 1% is Christian.[56] It is the last 'great frontier' for Christianity.

Who are these Muslims? We need to recognize that they are people just like you and me. They have the same concerns for their families as we do: paying bills, keeping jobs, raising their children, concern that their children are losing traditional values, concern about terrorism and violence, and concern for their well-being – just like us. They are people with a commitment to their God.[57] They believe in the one true, sovereign, almighty God who created heaven and earth and who will judge all humankind in the end. They have a devotion that puts some of us to shame. They esteem Jesus whom they see as the nearest one to God, but have trouble with the incarnation and with the crucifixion. They are like Peter in Matthew 16. Jesus asked, 'Who do men say that I am?' Peter answered, 'You are the Christ the son of the living God'. Jesus, afterward proceeded to tell him that he is going to be rejected, scourged and killed. Peter said,

---

[56] Again, these were the numbers in 1987.

[57] Both Arlene and Dr Douglas believed strongly that the God the Muslims sought to address was the same God as Jews and Christians know. As an Old Testament scholar, I recognize that linguistically, the Arabic form of *Allah* is the parallel form of *El* or *Elohim*. What I believe is missing in the Muslim belief system (as it was with the Canaanite neighbors of Israel who also recognized El as the high god) was a revelation of *Allah* or *Elohim* as *Yahweh*, who revealed Himself in a personal way to the world through Israel. Since Islam missed this revelation, they have also missed the incarnation, where Jesus revealed the Father and is, Himself, *Yahweh* – the LORD.

'God forbid, this can never be'. Muslims are people, like Peter, believe they are defending the honor of God.

Muslims are people who are very near the kingdom. They are people who, in the main, have not come to understand all of the riches of Jesus, the love of God, a personal relationship with God and the security of salvation through grace. They are people who desperately need the gospel. They are people who play an important part in God's eternal purpose.

'Oh, that Ishmael might live before you'. God says, 'I will surely bless him'. Think what blessing means. 'I'm going to give him (Ishmael) a tentful of kids?' God's promise of blessing always encompasses so much more. 'I will bless Ishmael.'

The prophet Isaiah, in chapter 42, speaks first of One who won't break a bruised reed, writes about the Suffering Servant, Jesus, then turns into joyous praise to God. In that praise the cities of the desert will praise God's name; and the people of Kedar, one of the sons of Ishmael, will join in. Isaiah lists a person, place, and tribe. Muslim interpreters of the scripture tell us that the place is Mecca. Yet, that passage in Isaiah 42 says the day is coming when they will sing the praises of the Servant who has come – will praise God for the sending of Jesus, God's servant, who served most admirably by his death and resurrection.

Isaiah 19 speaks of a day coming when the people of Egypt will come together with allegiance to the Lord. There will be a highway from Egypt to Assyria and they, along with Israel will worship the Lord – together, they will be a blessing on the earth. Isaiah uses words with them that he used for his special people, Israel. He calls them 'my people, my handiwork, my inheritance'. Isaiah says the day is coming when people in those areas of the world, which today are Muslim, will come to that kind of common faith. God is not through with Islam.

You and I need not fear Islam. We do need to be concerned if we find ourselves caught up in indifference and neglect. Muslim peoples are coming to faith in Christ. Just a few.[58] Someday, in the not too

---

[58] Since this was written many more Muslims have been coming to faith. Notable among them is Nabeel Qureshi, a Pakistani-American who, after his own radical conversion, became a notable apologist and paved the way for many other Muslims to find Jesus. See Nabeel Qureshi and Lee Strobel, *Seeking Allah, Finding Jesus* (Grand Rapids: Zondervan, 2018).

distant future those occasional droplets in the desert will become a shower and a thunderstorm and streams will begin to flow as thousands come to faith in Jesus Christ. Do we want to be involved in it or not? The starting point is awareness, and struggling with our own hearts and with our own prejudices.

The church has always been prejudiced. It took spectacular miracles to shake the early Christians out of its prejudice against non-Jews. Through the ages the church has always struggled with prejudice. Somehow being a 'new' person in Christ says we've made some progress. In 2 Cor. 5.16 Paul says.

> From now on, therefore, we regard no one according to the flesh. Even though we once regarded Christ according to the flesh, we regard him thus no longer. Therefore, if anyone is in Christ, he is a new creation.

Getting rid of the old and embracing the new means, I no longer view people from a worldly point of view. I begin to shed my prejudices, my fears, my de-humanization of the Muslims, and my shoving them aside so I can ignore them. Christians have to wrestle with these things! Awareness is where we start. We must wrestle with the issue of the old having gone and the new creation coming, in terms of how we look at and evaluate people. The new creation in Christ Jesus will struggle to set aside the old prejudices to look honestly at the constrictions we feel – praying and grappling with those constrictions, meeting, befriending and reaching them. They will know how we really view them.

When Israel left Sinai, it was a 10-day march to the Promised Land. With the choices Israel had made, operating out of fear, it took 40 years. Muslims *will* come into the kingdom of God. There's no question about it. The question is, 'Will it be a 10-day journey or a 40-year journey?'

We need to look at our fears, our motives, our love, our bravery. We need to look at how we respond to Muslims. We can be partners with God, or miss out on the blessing and let someone else get it.[59]

---

[59] Arlene had a great appreciation for Dr Douglas' teaching, mentoring, and friendship.

APPENDIX C

A Brief History of Islam and Its Founder Muhammad

With the Zwemer seminar copious notes in front of her, Arlene plunged right in. If students dropped a pencil, she said they lost a whole page of notes! Here, she is much indebted to Dr Douglas.

Dr Douglas began by teaching about Muhammad: his life and role in Muslim life; the Qur'an, its origin and nature, the place of tradition, the development of Islamic law (*sharia*) and the five pillars of Islam – how Islam is lived day by day by Muslims.[60]

He looked first at Muhammad and his role in Muslim life. It is important for the Christian worker to understand the centrality of Muhammad to Muslim thought and practice. Dr Douglas explained that to assume that you can understand Islam without knowing something about Muhammad's life and activities would be like trying to understand Christianity without knowing about the life of Jesus. Muhammad's activities present, in many ways, a model for the development of Islam in the life of the Muslim.

Muhammad was born in 570 CE and died in 632 CE. He was a grown man before he had his first supernatural experience, which he believed was from God. His public ministry lasted about 30 years and was divided between Mecca and Medina. In Mecca he basically played the role of a street preacher, offering critical comment on the religious practice of the people of Mecca. In 622 CE he left Mecca and moved to Medina. In Medina his role changed. He basically became a political organizer and eventually brought Islam to the point of dominating the religious life of Medina. From there, he began to harass the religious life of Mecca until he succeeded in overcoming them militarily, politically, and socially. He died suddenly in 632 without any apparent successor.

Muhammad was familiar with both Christian and Jewish traditions. He traveled a lot, and as he traveled, he heard stories. He

---

[60] Telephone conversation, December 14, 2018.

received his revelation[61] in seizures and dreams, but mostly he would go to a cave to pray where he would go into a trance.

He was married to several women. Hadiji, who was much older than he, was the one who influenced him the most. Hadiji convinced Muhammad that his dreams and seizures were from God, though at first, he doubted it.

Muhammad traveled as a merchant throughout the Middle East, up even into Israel where he met with Christian Jesuits with whom he camped out. He met many other Jewish people and they conversed together. He himself was unlearned, but he learned much about the Jews and their beliefs and about Jerusalem in these discussions. Many things in the Qur'an were influenced by them, but many things were not biblical because he got most of his information second-hand from these traveling companions. For example, he wrote that Miriam was the wife of Moses. Muhammad said he, himself, went to the seventh heaven (outdoing Paul who said that he was taken to the third heaven.) Muhammad did believe that Miriam gave birth to Jesus (Issa or Assa) and that she was a virgin. Jews don't believe this, but Muslims do, and they believe that Jesus was a great prophet.

---

[61] Muhammad's first revelation was an event described in Islam as taking place in 610 CE. It was during that event that the Islamic prophet, Muhammad, was visited by the angel, Jibril, known as Gabriel in English, who revealed to him the beginnings of what would later become the Qur'an.

APPENDIX D

Muslim Social Institutions – Sunni and Shia

Included in Zwemer teaching would be some attention to Muslim social institutions such as the mosque, schools, charitable institutions, denominations and political expression. Islam developed a variety of denominations – two major groups – the Sunni and the Shia. The Sunni's are divided according to schools of interpretation. The Shia are divided into at least three major denominations. The initial division between Shia and Sunni was over who should succeed Muhammad. Later the factor that came into play was the question, 'What do you look to in order to decide what God wants you to do?' The Sunni would say you look to the Qur'an and the traditions, or you look to what is written. The Shia would say, you look to the Qur'an and the traditions; but you also seek the living voice of God, and you find the living voice of God in the successor of Muhammad. Their view of who the successor of Muhammad was is very different from the Sunni. So, you almost have a similar kind of Protestant-Catholic tradition here.

In Iran, for example, Khomeini was elevated to be the Ayatollah by fellow leaders within the Iranian branch of Islam. It's almost like the practice of how do you go about choosing the Pope. You would say that the College of Cardinals does it, usually choosing one of its own members. It is similar in Islam: the Ayatollah is chosen by people who are his peers, people of the upper leadership of Islam.

Khomeini was not the successor to Muhammad, but as Ayatollah, he was as close to that as you could get in modern Islam. There are smaller groups of Sunni and Shia within the two major groups, and the divisions have come mostly concerning the issue of 'who is the descendant of Muhammad'.[62]

Vital to all Muslims is the Qur'an. The students of the Qur'an describe its coming into existence gradually over a number of years as Muhammad encountered various situations and felt that God was

---

[62] Telephone conversation with Dr Douglas, December 14, 2018.

telling him how to respond to those situations. Part of the Qur'an was 'revealed' during Muhammad's time in Mecca. The emphasis during that time was largely upon the importance of a moral and devout life and the Oneness of God. Much of the Qur'an came to Muhammad during his days in Medina. The latter emphasis shifts to instructions concerning the community, as a community of faith and how it needs to behave. The latter part includes particular statements against those who were opposing Muhammad and his ideas. Some Muslims believe all of the Qur'an was revealed to Muhammad in a very brief time. Others recognize that its units came together over a much longer period of time. In fact, the Qur'an was not gathered into one volume until a couple of decades after the death of Muhammad.

What about the place of tradition? In the actual practice of Islam, tradition plays a bigger role than the Qur'an. Tradition developed gradually and is usually attributed to actions or activities to be found in association with the life of Muhammad. In reality, most traditions came a considerable time after Muhammad. At a practical level, tradition probably determines the shape and attitude of the life of the Muslim more than the Qur'an. For example, the Qur'an does not specify prayer five times a day. This arose out of tradition. Today in some Muslim circles, the value and even legitimacy of the traditions are being questioned.

Islamic law is based on the Qur'an and on the traditions and decisions of memorable Muslim judges in the early centuries of Islam's existence. Islamic law encompasses most areas of life, including political activity, commerce, religious practice, and economics. Islamic law *in its totality* is not practiced anywhere in the Muslim world. There is no one place or book where all of Islamic law is found. Different countries and governments include different portions of *sharia* in the laws of that particular nation. *Sharia* is the Islamic equivalent of Islamic law which means 'the way' or 'the pathway'. The most complete application of Islamic law would be in the Iranian peninsula and Saudi Arabia, but even there it is not consistently followed. The interpretation of *sharia* is left to notable religious scholars. Who would be included in that list of important people would vary from place to place. In some places, religious scholars of 500 years ago might be appealed to, while in other places, notable scholars of today might be appealed to.

APPENDIX E

Islamic Theology

The third major section of Arlene's teaching would introduce her students to Islamic theology. This includes the Muslim's concept of God, prophets, revelation and scripture, sin and salvation, and the end times. I (Marcia) would recommend Phil Parshall's book, *Understanding Muslim Teachings and Traditions*[63] concerning theology, though now there are many other good books available. Much of what follows is from his book.

For the Muslim it is important that God is absolutely a unity. 'Allah has no partners and has no resemblance to anything whatsoever in any respect'. By this they are strongly denying the Christian view of Father, Son, and Holy Spirit as all being uniquely and mysteriously God (p. 9); he is the all omnipotent one. Allah will always operate within the perimeters of his will (p. 65).

'To Muslims, Muhammad's words and deeds are as fresh, vital and binding in the present as they were when first spoken more than thirteen hundred years ago' (p. 39). Concerning revelation, 'The Qur'an sets forth its existence as ultimate truth' (p. 18).

Sin is very real to the Muslim. Prayer is key to obtaining forgiveness of sin (p. 63). Cleansing, prayer, and forgiveness come together (p. 64).

Personal salvation is important to Muslims. They believe in the eternal existence of the soul as Christians do. The process of salvation is a key theme in all Islamic scripture.

There are five pillars of Islam: *shahada:* faith; *salah:* prayer (five times a day); *zakat:* charity; *sawm:* fasting; *hajj:* pilgrimage to Mecca.

Faith is even more important than good works. 'Without a firm and unshakable faith in the God of truth and his word, the Qur'an, there can be no salvation for the Muslim' (p. 33).

---

[63] Phil Parshall, *Understanding Muslim Teachings and Traditions: A Guide for Christians* (Grand Rapids, MI: Baker Books, 1994). Page references to Phil Parshall's book will follow each statement of belief.

Prayer is the human response to the omnipotence of God (p. 63). By it people accumulate merit, especially in groups. Prayer is efficacious for cancelling one's sins (p. 64). Prayer is 'simply getting ourselves and our desires in concert with the will of Allah to accept what Allah has ordained for us' (p. 65).

Fasting is only a fast during daylight. They don't eat until the sun goes down and they eat early in the morning before the sun comes up. There are strong regulations concerning sexual relationships during the fast (p. 78). Fasting is connected with deprivation, rewards, and joy (p. 77).

The *hajj* is considered the apex of religious experience. It is an obligation for all Muslims to travel to Mecca at least once (p. 84). Kissing the Black Stone is central to the *hajj* ritual. It is not considered to be magic but is simply following the example of Muhammad as an act of faith (p. 87). The simple dress of the *hajj* makes everyone equal (p. 88).

They believe that there is a scale weighing their good deeds against the bad deeds. If their good deeds outweigh the bad deeds they can go to paradise. Of course, they need to have kept the five pillars to be considered good. Muslims also believe strongly in hell. If you go to hell, it is like wearing a coat of burning pitch. When that coat burns off you get another coat of pitch and this continues forever. Of course, if they are killed in a holy war (*jihad*) they automatically go to heaven where they will have 70 virgins. They believe there are angels in heaven.

APPENDIX F

Muslim/Arab Customs and Traditions

The fourth major area would be to focus on the cultural aspects of Islam. This would involve obtaining a view of the Muslim world, giving special attention to values that are found in all Muslim cultures. These values include the importance of the community as opposed to the individual, hospitality, and the special place of honor and shame.

The importance of community, wherever you find it in Muslim culture, tends to be group-oriented; and the extended family is far more important than the individual. Decisions are usually made within the family by the oldest males. This creates a problem for us in the West when we try to minister to Muslims because we tend to be very individualistic. This sets up a conflict which is very difficult to resolve.[64]

In Dr Douglas' opinion, honor and shame stand at the very center of Islamic cultures. Honor has to do with the reputation of the group – the reputation of the individual is always seen as a part of that group's reputation. Honor-shame determines multitudes of actions in life. How do you greet people? How do you welcome them? How do you deal with disagreements? How do you express sorrow and anger? A kind of example was an instance in which Dr Douglas remembers saying to an acquaintance, 'Will you come to my home?' His potential guest felt he must decline. He declined, not by saying, 'I don't want to' or 'I can't,' but, by saying, 'I don't want to trouble you'. I said, 'It's no trouble'. If I had continued to press, he would agree to come, but in actual fact, he wouldn't come. Later, when I saw him and asked about it, he would say, 'My uncle died'. It would not be clear whether that was an actual event or not, but it would be an accepted explanation because obligation to family always takes precedence. That's the way he excuses himself and maintains honor

---

[64] This section is also thanks to Dr Douglas in telephone conversation, December 14, 2018.

and does not dishonor me. You may find these kinds of dynamics almost feel like a game or play, but it is far more serious than that. In terms of ministry, this has some serious implications.

The implications of each of these cultural aspects for effective communication with Muslims would be analyzed. When do you talk about the Gospel and how you talk about it? You do not attack Muhammad or the Qur'an. To do so is to dishonor these very revered entities and the result would be a complete collapse of communication. From a western perspective, we simply want to attack these by saying things like, 'Muhammad was immoral or imposter', or 'the Qur'an was a human production'. There are ways one can talk without violating honor-shame: this is by telling stories. There are incredible similarities with the Christian world, but we often lose sight of or ignore them. For example, Jesus told stories. An example from the Old Testament is how Nathan confronted David about his sin. He did not attack; instead, he told a story which enabled David to judge himself.

Another major component would be to focus on folk Islam, that is, Islam as influenced by concepts of magic, impersonal powers, and spirit beings such as saints, ancestors, and demons. They believe in the *jinn*.[65] Some analysis of how to address these matters would be part of the study of this unit.

Bible Customs

Some Muslim customs come from the Bible. For instance, Muslims need to slaughter their meat in a certain way. They slit the throat and drain it of all the blood, just as the Old Testament prescribes. The meat that is safe is called *halal*.[66]

Hospitality

One of the people in the Bible they really revere is Abraham and especially his hospitality. Water is very precious in the Middle East, but in Aboud it was not required to always give water upon entering a house as it is in many places like South Sudan. Of course, one

---

[65] In Muslim demonology it is an intelligent spirit of lower rank than angels, able to appear in human and animal forms and to possess humans.

[66] The remainder of the section is from the memory of Arlene, herself.

should be willing to provide it, if asked. The people in Aboud had to go to the valley to get their water at great trouble. In later years they had water piped in. It was important at Aboud to always give visitors coffee and chocolate.

Superstitions

One custom that was really new to Arlene was that you never show the bottom of your feet to any Arab. To do so would mean, 'You are nothing but the dirt under my feet'. Other superstitions include what one would say in the event of the birth of a child. You never say, 'Oh, that's a beautiful baby'. They are afraid of the 'evil eye', both Muslim and Christian Arabs. You would say '*smallah*,' in the name of God, to protect them from the evil eye.

Because they believe that blue is good luck, the iron of the windows of their homes are typically some shade of blue. They also put horseshoes on the door decorated with blue beads. They even put blue beads on the babies to keep the 'evil eye' away.

Handling The Qur'an

Muslims are proud of having only one version of the Qur'an; and, of course, it is in Arabic, which is considered the holy language. Though Muhammad was unlearned, many people believe the Angel Gabriel gave him word for word what to write. Since they reverence the book so much, they would never lay the Qur'an on the floor, or lay anything on it, and they would wash their hands before touching it. As Christians we should never put our holy book on the floor either or a lot of books on top of it if we are in the presence of Muslims.

Don't ever pick up a Muslim's Qur'an. Without thinking, Arlene reached forward to pick up one gentleman's Qur'an, saying, 'Oh, you're reading the Qur'an'. As she reached for the book, she saw the look on his face and realized, 'I'm an unholy Christian, a woman, and have not washed my hands'.

The Hajj

Women pray in a separate place in the mosque, but they can even go on the *hajj*. Women who have gone on the *hajj* are called *hajji*. The men are called *hajj*. It's very expensive, so a lot of people don't get to go. For a Muslim man or woman, it is regarded as a trip of a lifetime, much as a Christian esteems a trip to the Holy Land.

APPENDIX G

A Partial Listing of Students from the Missionary Training Center in São Paulo, Brazil

Taught by Missionary Arlene Miller
1994-2009[67]

Rodolfo and Monica Guerra	Argentina	1994	Pastor and pioneer church planter in northern Argentina; missions mobilizer.
Vilma Almirón	Argentina	1994	Served as a District and National Missions leader in Argentina. Studied nursing in Argentina and also studied in Manila in the Philippines. Serves as a missionary to Thailand with her husband Erick Estevez from Honduras, working with the sex trafficking trade to free young women.
Gustavo José Chavez	Argentina	1995	Served as a Regional Missions leader, professor at CTM, and pastor of a local church in São Paulo. Served with his wife Mariani in Spain for 12 years; Gustavo completed a doctorate from Dallas Seminary in missions. He is currently the Director of CTM and the leader of the COG Latin American Missions Board (AEMI). Gustavo and Mariani also pastor a local church in São Paulo.
Alejandro Díaz Rodriguez	Chile	1996	Dynamic missions leader in Santiago, Chile; He served on both regional and national levels; Alejandro served as a member of the South American Missions Council. Led many groups of youth on short-term missions; Alejandro

---

[67] This information was collated and provided by John Hayes.

				has passed away. His surviving wife Isabel is also a graduate of CTM.
Karina M. Ramirez Petcoff	Argentina	1996		Graduated from Lee University with a Master in Education. Missionary to Bulgaria from 2000-2002, and now since 2009. Eventually married a Bulgarian pastor who serves as an assistant in a church in Stara Zagora, Bulgaria. Karina teaches in the Bible School and is involved in training leaders.
Josué Ruiz Zavaleta	Peru	1997		Fulfilled an internship of one year in Brazil where he and his wife Maribel helped to plant the church in Cajamar, São Paulo. Has served for many years as a missionary in Bolivia. He currently pastors in Cochabamba with his wife Maribel, also a graduate of CTM
Aguinaldo Alves França	Brasil	1998		Worked in Bolivia for a year and then for many years in Mozambique with Iris Ministries (Heidi Baker), leading the base in Pemba. Aguinaldo passed away on furlough in Brazil following a surgery.
Daniel Cirilo Leguizamón	Paraguay	1998		First missionary sent out by the COG in Paraguay, sent to plant churches in Bolivia, setting a great example with a dynamic ministry and church planting.
Gamaliel González Romero	Mexico	1998		Professor at SEMISUD in Quito, Ecuador
María Deisy Mina Ocoro	Ecuador	1998		Pastor and missionary in Ecuador
Abidoral da Silva	Brasil	1999		Planted the mother church in Boa Vista in the state of Roraima in Brazil near Venezuela; sent and supported by the SE Region of Brazil; currently pastors in Itaituba, Pará; He assists with missions to the Munduruku tribal group under the Arrowhead Project
Marcelo and Emma Rodríguez	Argentina	1999		Dynamic District, Regional, and National missions leader in Argentina. Influential in creating sending structures in the COG in

			Argentina. Husband of Emma Aranda Rodriguez (deceased).
Patricia Paredes Guerra	Chile	1999	Worked with Dr Luis Solis in Ceuta, Spain as a missionary nurse.
Fernando and Cristina Romera	Argentina	2000	Served as Coordinator at CTM in Brazil; Fernando and Cristina currently work as missionaries in Spain since 2011.
Roxana Rotela	Argentina	2000	Worked with the City of Refuge orphanage in São Paulo for her internship; Pastored with her Brazilian husband Samuel in São Paulo for many years; currently in the USA learning English before going to Mongolia.
Nivaldo and Maria Aparecida Ribeiro	Brasil	2001	Served as missionaries in Guatemala for one year and for eight years in Mozambique for their denomination. He currently serves as the Coordinator of CTM in São Paulo, Brazil together with Maria.
Santa Teresa Mamani	Chile	2001	Missionary sent by the churches in Chile to India where she serves since 2004 with her husband near Chennai leading an orphanage and training leaders by initiating a Bible School program. Her husband Samuel Dhanasekaris is a pastor from India.
Alejandra Zamudio	Argentina	2002	Worked with the City of Refuge in São Paulo, Brazil (2008), then with the Arrowhead Project in Santarém (2009-2010) and Manaus, Brazil 2011, 2014, 2016). She has also done short-term missions in South Africa (2015). Alejandra served in Senegal for two years (2017-19).
Ricardo Walter Gil	Argentina	2002	Serves with Youth With a Mission in Argentina
María 'Célia' Méndez dos Santos	Brasil	2003	'Celia' has been a missionary in Mozambique for many years since 2003, working with Iris Ministries (Heidi Baker) in the orphanage, and with the COG in establishing pastoral training. She is currently working to plant and build

			churches with the COGWM Firewall Project.
Suely Marinho Ferreira	Brasil	2003	Graduated with BA in Theology and Education. Served as a local missions leader and as the Vice-President of the Regional Missions Department for NE Brazil. She worked in India for 5 years until she had health issues; She is currently serving as a missions leader in her local church and for her State in NE Brazil.
Areli Fernando da Silva	Brasil	2004	Brazilian missionary serving as a pastor in Argentina
María Sol Romera	Argentina	2004	Served with her parents in São Paulo at CTM (Fernando and Cristina – CTM 2000) and made several trips to Spain; now married and currently lives in Mar del Plata in Argentina where she works with a literacy program (Letra Argentina) as a part of the Wycliff Global Alliance. She also is the National Coordinator of Mobilization within that agency. Her husband Natanael is also a son of missionaries (MK) that worked with the La Paz Mission among the Wichi Indigenous Tribe in northern Argentina. He worked with the agency Latin Link as a translator in England. He currently serves with the Bible Society of Argentina.
Francisca Gonzales Avalos	Paraguay	2005	Missionary sent to India for one year by the COG in Paraguay.
Vanesa Lazarte	Argentina	2005	Vanesa was sent to France by the COG in Argentina for several years (2007, 2008-2009): She continues to travel to Europe, Asia, and the USA working with the pastoral care of missionaries. She currently serves as a pastor in Buenos Aires, Argentina with her husband. She is the Regional Missions Director taking youth on short-term missions experiences. Her husband

			Alexander Hernandez is from Guatemala. Vanesa is also a representative of EIMI, the Latin American Missions Agency for the COG.
Allison Costa	Brasil	2009	Served for a period with Asas de Socorro (missionary aviation agency). Local missions leader and mobilizer in Altamira, Pará, Brazil with the Vineyard Church.
Iris Noemí Lopez Letona	Guatemala	2010	Bible School teacher in Guatemala; also served in Santarém, Pará, Brazil for one year in the Seminary
Keisiane Cavalcante Carvalho	Brasil	2010	Worked with the Arrowhead Project and the Munduruku tribal group in Pará, Brazil for two years. Currently lives with her husband in Idaho.
Lucenildo and Andreina Silva Lima	Brasil	2010	Lucenildo worked with the Arrowhead Project in Manaus and with the Munduruku tribe in the state of Pará. Lucenildo and Andreina recently planted a church in Vitória do Xingú, Pará. They continue to be involved in the ministry to the tribal groups through the Arrowhead Project.
María Rosemary Beserra	Brasil	2010	Missionary to Portugal for her denomination

APPENDIX H[68]

Curricula at the Missionary Training Center

Theology of Missions
This study focuses on the Bible basis of missions, beginning with the missionary character of God and concluding with the multi-cultural multitude around the throne in heaven. This subject endeavors to give the student a panoramic view of God's plan of redemption as well as the purpose in reaching all the people groups of the world. It analyzes each book of the Bible, beginning with the missionary plan of God in the Old Testament using Israel as an instrument. The plan of God to use the multi-cultural church in the New Testament is studied.

History of Missions
The study of the history of missions demonstrates the various periods and missionary movements. It includes an analysis of past errors, as well as the positive contributions of the missionary effort. The purpose of this study is that the Latin American missionaries might avoid the historical errors of the past, as well as benefit from the experience of those groups that have had more experience in cross-cultural ministry.

Missionary Life and Character
This is a study of the calling, spiritual gifting, personality, character, family, conflicts, relationships, and specific problems relating to the missionary. It includes an analysis of the symptoms, dangers, and solutions for cultural shock so that missionary candidates will be prepared to face it in the future. The class includes spiritual gift testing and an analysis of the various personality types. It endeavors to prepare the student for the reality of cross-cultural ministry, demonstrating the various elements of missionary life and cross-cultural ministry.

Cultural Anthropology
Cultural anthropology is the study of the cultural forms within various societies, demonstrating the purpose and value of culture. This

---

[68] Written and provided by John Hayes and represents the curricula under which Arlene taught.

subject strives to prepare the missionary to observe, understand, and participate in the worldview, values, and behavior of a different culture. The purpose of this training is to enable the student to utilize contextualized forms in the evangelization of other cultures.

Spiritual Warfare
Spiritual Warfare is the study of the Scriptures, biblical methods, strategies, and practice of spiritual warfare for the purpose of defeating spiritual forces within the culture, city, and country, enabling the gospel to have access to human hearts.

Linguistic Techniques
The purpose of this study is not primarily that of learning linguistic theory, but to study the practical application of techniques which enable a missionary to learn the language and culture more efficiently and rapidly. Practical suggestions are offered, and students are given an opportunity to learn another language while studying at the Center.

Contextualization and Adaptation
This study demonstrates the contextualization of the message, the messenger, and the methods of communication within each culture. It includes practical suggestions in how to adapt and integrate into another culture, identifying with the people of the host culture. Past and present errors that missionaries have made are discussed.

Observation-Participant
This study teaches the missionary candidate how to observe a culture and cultural behavior, learning culture in a manner which leads to participation and identification with the people. The methods are applied in a practical setting.

Missionary Strategy and Methodology
This course is an analysis of the Biblical strategy of missions from a Pentecostal perspective delineating principles which can be applied to any culture. The need to adapt and contextualize each method within the distinct culture is emphasized, and various examples of modern and creative methods are demonstrated. Strategies and methods of reaching various people groups are a part of this study.

The Local Church and Missions

This is a study of the mutual responsibility between the missionary and the local church. The missionary is prepared to develop the missions vision within the local church through teaching and participation. Methods and means of communicating with the sending churches are discussed.

Urban Missiology

Since one of the major challenges of future missionary work is the ministry within rapidly growing urban areas, this subject prepares students to form strategies and contextualized ministries to those living in urban areas.

Specific Studies

Each student develops a strategy including objectives and goals, contextualized methods, and a working plan directed toward a specific people group. These studies are directed toward the group that the student feels called to, such as the Muslim peoples. This study may be subjected to an oral evaluation by professors or a designated committee.

Introduction to Islam

This is a study which endeavors to awaken interest in reaching the Muslim world. A basic analysis of the Islam faith is provided, and contextualized methods are discussed. Students are prepared to evangelize Muslims within Latin America and throughout the world.

Optional courses

Other courses were taught from time to time and the curriculum also included orientation periods, weekly meetings for reflection, personal and pastoral counseling, psychological counseling and analysis with a professional Christian psychologist, internships and ministerial experiences within a cross-cultural setting, short-term experiences in a cross-cultural setting, group devotional periods, one-on-one contact with missionaries on the field, intensive training courses, conferences and retreats, and daily contact with people of other cultures.

www.ingramcontent.com/pod-product-compliance
Lightning Source LLC
LaVergne TN
LVHW020933090426
835512LV00020B/3340